𝔘𝔩𝔩𝔲𝔪𝔦𝔫𝔞𝔱𝔦 𝔑𝔢𝔴𝔰 𝔓𝔯𝔢𝔰𝔢𝔫𝔱𝔰:

Dialogue with "Hidden Hand", Self-Proclaimed Illuminati Insider

by Wes Penre, Illuminati News, Dec 27, 2008

THE HIDDEN HAND

MOTHER ✱ TEACHER ✦ DESTROYER

This self-proclaimed illuminati [def] Insider appeared on the "Above Top Secret" forum in October 2008, giving away information about the Illuminati Agenda and their goals. The reason for this, he says, is because time is right for us to know some of what is going on behind the scenes. And when he explains WHY he needs to reveal it now, it's very convincing. In this article I will post the dialogue between the "Above Top Secret Forum" members and "Hidden Hand" in its entirety.

Please take time to read through this whole dialogue (yes, I know it's long, but I think we all can benefit from it, even if you end up not believing what is said). When you read it, you need to have an open mind; you can't be stuck in dogma or think you "have it all figured out" already, because then it doesn't matter what he says, you won't believe it.

Here are some points which makes him very believable; one being that the forum members he is communicating with make up pages after pages of random questions (as you can see in this article) and he answers them intelligently and precisely without the delay it would take for a person presenting a hoax to come up with them. This is also what the forum members notice. And he is consistent! Many of the questions are very good, deep, to the point and philosophical, and this guy (or woman, we don't know - this being claims not to be from this Earth), manages to reply on a very deep level, and his answers don't contradict each other. In an advanced and intelligent dialogue like this, it's very unlikely anyone would be able to do that without giving himself away at some point. You will most certainly notice he/she is sincere.

Ever wondered who is "on top of the Pyramid?" He gives us a clue. The bloodline he represents is well above the Rothschild's in power and in the hierarchy and is extra-terrestrial in origin. The 13 bloodlines we have been talking about thus far on this website and others, with the Rothschild's in a top position together with the Merovingian Nobility, are quite low rank in the Big Pyramid Structure, and are the ones playing a power game here on Earth, only aware of parts of the Big Game (a need to know basis). The bloodline "Hidden Hand" is supposedly belonging to is way more advanced and higher rank.

I really think this being believes in what he is saying, and whether he is deceived himself to some degree or not, this is most probably what is driving the Illuminati. These are their goals! It leaves you with a pretty strange feeling after have read it all, but deep inside it rings true.

His answers may need to be read more than once to understand the different layers of what he is telling us. Afterwards, when you start connecting the dots you notice that a lot of pieces in the big puzzle that previously were missing and left unanswered, suddenly fit.

If you are visiting the Illuminati News website for the first time, already have a fair concept of what the Illuminati and the New World Order is about, and you only intend to read ONE article from my huge database, I would say this one would be the one to read!

It's been hard to perceive what ULTIMATELY drives the Illuminati. Greed? Yes. Power? Of course.

Control? Sure. But you always have this feeling that there is a deeper mystery behind their "Great Work of the Ages". This may very well be the answer!

When you are done reading this article and feel inspired, please go to the website, Law of One, and start absorbing the information presented there. It is a huge database on the same subject, but extensively expanded. Both these article, may if we read them with understanding plus an open mind and an open heart, show us the real so[u]lution to the New World Order [def] problem.

Here is the dialogue between the Above Top Secret members [ATS] and "Hidden Hand" [HH], the self-proclaimed Illuminati Insider (the emphases in **bold** throughout the article are mine to separate out certain keys points I want to highlight):

First Session:

HH: I am a generational member of a Ruling Bloodline Family.

Every so often, as per the directives of the Law of our Creator, a brief window of opportunity opens, whereby a select handful of our Family are required to make communication with our subjects, and offer you the chance to ask us any questions you would like answered.

I am double-bound in this duty. It is required of me by The Law of our Creator to offer this opportunity to you at this time, though I am also bound by the Law of (planetary) Free Will and by Family Oaths, that there is only so much I am able to say.

Rules define life in games.

If you wish to participate, here they are:

1). I will afford you courtesy and respect in the manner I address you, and I expect the same from you in reciprocation.

2). I will decide whether or not I am either willing or permitted to answer your question. If your question is not answered, it is either because I cannot disclose it, or because I considered your question was lacking in one or more of the following: respect, courtesy, intelligence, decency, or that it was otherwise unworthy of being dignified with a response.

3). That you agree to treat this potential dialogue with an aspect of "provisional faith". In practice, this means that rather than impeding the flow of information with crass comments of disbelief or petty name calling, my participation here requires of you that you discourse with me under "suspended judgment". In other words, wait until the process is complete, before deciding for yourself as to the content of truth and knowledge imparted herein.

4). That you formulate your questions intelligently. My time is limited. I do not want to waste it by having to trawl through pointless, futile, insensible or disrespectful questions, therefore I will answer the questions I feel are most deserving of a response, during the time that I have available. Use the time we have wisely.

If any of the above conditions are breached, I reserve the right to terminate our discourse forthwith, if I so choose.

That being said, I will attempt to answer your questions as honestly and openly as is permissible for me. I will check back and respond as time allows.

ATS: How many generations back does your bloodline extend, or, perhaps more accurately, who does your family consider its earliest ancestor in a position of power?

HH: Our Lineage can be traced back beyond antiquity. From the earliest times of your recorded "history", and beyond, our Family has been 'directing' the 'play' from behind the scenes, in one way or another. Before the rise and fall of Atlantis. (Yes, that was indeed perfectly real). We are 'born to lead'. It is part of the design for this current paradigm.

ATS: To what extent has selective breeding been used to preserve the purity of the line? and what becomes of children of unapproved unions? (They would naturally still be raised with privilege, but not, perhaps "given the keys to the castle" as it were?)

HH: The breeding is generally case specific, dependant upon the role that the Family members in question are due to grow into. I will touch more on this in answer to the next poster's question that you rephrased.

There are no unapproved unions. Our Family will always intermarry between lines, or, what we would term 'Houses' [1]. Marriages are arranged. In all my years alive, I have never seen or heard of a Family member breaking this code, as far as marriage goes. You do as you are told. One cannot 'join' the Family. One is 'born', or incarnated into it.

On the rare instances of a child being born that could be seen as bringing 'difficulties', you are correct in your premise, that it would be raised as part of the Family, though would not grow up in the house or community of either of it's parents.

ATS: If one were to imagine a scale, perhaps as a triangle with Political, Religious and Corporate power at the three points, how would you categorize the power your family yields? (Balanced? Leaning more towards one or two than a third? Heavily favoring one of the three above the others?) And has that position shifted over time?

HH: You need to first understand the structure of the Family. In the grand scheme of things, the Line is not as important as the House, the House, is not as important as the Family. The Family is all. No matter the House or Line, we are One (truly international) Family.

Imagine if you will, **a** body. A House would represent a vital organ or body part within the Body itself. Each part has an important role to play in the functioning of the whole, and to each of us, the 'whole' has our undivided loyalty. As I say, many lines, (far more than you are aware of), One Family.

Our realms of influence do not fit as comfortably into the three boxes of your triangle as you may imagine. There are **six disciplines of training within the Family**, and each member of the Family is schooled extensively in all of them, from early childhood. We all have an area of specialty, though we have experience in all spheres. The six spheres or 'schools' of learning are **Military, Government, Spiritual, Scholarship, Leadership, and Sciences**. In practice, out there on the 'stage' of public life, **we hold key positions in all of these main areas of importance**. With the **addition of** a complicit **Media** machine and ownership of your **Financial establishments**, all bases are covered.

I will have to reply in parts, due to the restriction of characters per post.

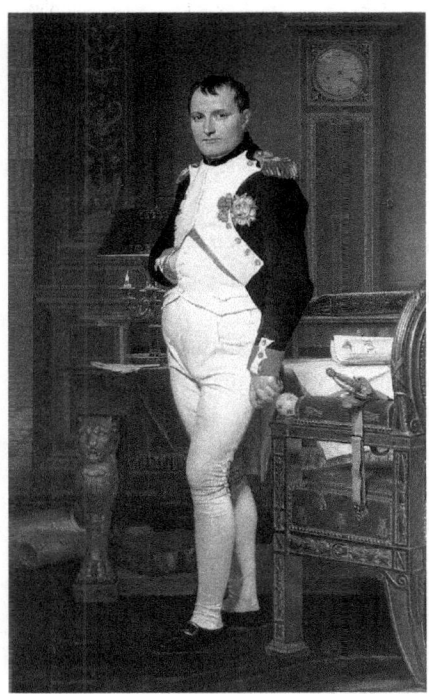

Napoleon making the "Hidden Hand" sign, showing off that he is "initiated"

ATS: Which Ruling Bloodline Family.... Rockefellers?

That may be a bit too direct for our inquisitee. I'd offer the following substitute:

How many parallel bloodlines do you estimate are in similar positions to your own, and to what extent does your family see them as either competition or collaborators?

HH: Yes, as I say, knowing the line is of no practical use to you. It is the belonging to the Family that is important.

There are **13 'base' or 'core' original bloodlines**. Yet there are **many many other lines** that **spring from these**, as do rivers from the oceans. If you imagine the 13 Original lines as Primary colour, that can be mixed to create a vast array of other colours, then you will have some comprehension. Again, no competition, just Family.

No competition in the sense of House against House, though it is a 'dog eat dog' world. So there is interpersonal competition in that sense of the word. Everyone wants to move up. Our whole Familial society is geared that way, toward upward progression.

ATS: What does the term " generational member" mean? Which generation specifically?

HH: It means that one is born into the Family. The Order and it's agenda is handed down, from generation to generation. Only in extremely rare occasions, have outsiders been invested into the Family, and then, even these were of other 'esoterically' integrable lines.

ATS: Can you cite two or more previous instances whereby this directive has been upheld?

HH: Once in 1999, to what you would call an 'alternative' media source. Once in 2003, on another internet "conspiracy" based forum. Though the information relayed was not entirely 'pure'. Not from the intention of misleading, but rather through imperfect or incomplete knowledge of the messengers.

If it is not in the mainstream controlled media, it will not be believed by the masses. This is information tailored for those who already know that we are very real, and exerting a strong, if mostly subtle, influence over your lives. If you wish to enslave a man, allow him to believe that he is already free.

ATS: By what basis is the timing of such revelations established?

HH: By the decree of the **Supreme World Council**, according to the Will of the Creator.

ATS: Are we really considered chattel and traded as such by the government?

HH: By the governments, generally, yes. People are seen as 'collateral'. Pawns that are maneuvered around the chess board, according to the game plan. By the Family, contrary to popular beliefs, **many of us do not mean you any harm directly**. There is just the matter of divine destiny to uphold and unfold, and we must play our parts in the game, as given to us by the Creator. In many ways, it is actually **in our own interest that you are prepared for the coming Harvest. Just not maybe prepared in quite the way that you would like**. Still, even then, you are choosing the Negative Polarity with your own Free Will decisions, with a little 'help' and direction from us. Souls are Harvestable in either 'extreme' of the Polarities, one could say.

ATS: If so, how do we become freemen?

HH: You will never be 'free', for as long as you are incarnating on this planet. The very nature of your being here, is indication of that. There is a reason why you are here, and 'here' is very likely not really where you think 'here' is. How do you become free? By working out where you are, and coming to an understanding, of why you are here [2]. **You are fast running out of time to do so, before the coming Harvest. Those that don't make it, will have to repeat the cycle**.

ATS: Is the Messiah alive today?

HH: There is no "Messiah". Stop looking outside of yourself for 'salvation'.

Is there what you might call a 'Christ Consciousness' alive, then yes, in a manner of speaking. Though not in your 3rd Density (dimensional) awareness.

ATS: Is it the **end-times, as described in the book of revelations?**

HH: Yes. Not just described in the Book of Revelations, but also in the prophesies of virtually every religion, spiritual philosophy, and mystery tradition throughout history. **This time is now at hand.**

To use your own example however:

Revelation 14:14-16:

14 Then I looked, and behold, a white cloud, and on the cloud sat One like the Son of Man, having on His head a golden crown, and in His hand a sharp sickle. 15 And another angel came out of the temple, crying with a loud voice to Him who sat on the cloud, "Thrust in Your sickle and reap, for the time has come for You to reap, for the harvest of the earth is ripe." 16 So He who sat on the cloud thrust in His sickle on the earth, and the earth was reaped.

The 'earth' is indeed ripe for Harvest. The question is, who will be ready? And will the Harvest be Positive, or Negative?

ATS: How do you justify that the current British royal family line is the true bloodline, but Ishmael is not the true receiver of Abraham's gift? If you're true bloodline, you'll know what I mean.

HH: Who says it is the 'true' line? **There were Ruling-Bloodlines long before your 'Yahweh' and his 'Christianity' arrived on this planet. Yahweh is 'a' Creator, not 'The' One Infinite Creator. There are other and Higher 'gods' than him.** Ultimately, All, are a part of The One, and either consciously, or unconsciously, exercising their Free Will to Create. **Begin to study 'outside of the box'** for a True understanding of the Creation.

The British Royalty is not the most powerful line. The names that you know, do not hold the real ancient power. **There are others above these lineages in the Hierarchy.** You will not know the names of these lines.

ATS: OP, what proof do you have that "ruling elite families" exist and that your a member of one? Its something that I think you thought was not falsifiable, which is why you chose that identity for the story your weaving - however, I think there may indeed be a way you can prove it.

HH: I have no need to prove anything to you. I am merely doing my duty as directed to me. Believe, or do not believe, we are divinely indifferent. I am obliged to complete this task here. The end result is of no consequence to me. I will have discharged my duty, in handing down certain information that must be released at this time. There is no stipulation as to where I do so, only that I do. I chose Above Top Secret, as the general level of intelligence, comprehension and reasoning is reckoned to be higher than in many such forums.

Understand, due to the Law of Free Will, I cannot just give you information, at least not without consequences to my own person which I would rather avoid. It is an infringement upon your Free Will, your right to not know. You have to ask me for the information you want, only then can I provide it. So whilst there are important things I have to share, if I am not asked the questions, I cannot get that information to you. I am hopeful that synchronicity will bring the most important questions of real 'depth' out from among you.

My duty is to offer. Yours is to ask. My duty is fulfilled, whether or not yours is.

ATS: Surely if ruling elite families exist and your a member of one then you must be controlling global events through world governments - tell us 1 major government action from any country that going to occur in the next 5 days.

I won't be surprised when you refuse to do so.

HH: [*on Sept. 10, 2008*]: I am not at liberty to discuss such intimate immediate detail, and in many cases, I am not far enough up the Hierarchy to know anyway. Typically, I would receive a call a day before the enactment of a major event, just to say something along the lines of 'this part of such and such a plan will take place tomorrow, in such and such a way, do not be alarmed'. Also one has to take into account, the specific areas of specialty I mentioned previously. My area is in Spirituality, so my focus is not so much on Geo-Political events. I am aware of the overall design, though the finer points are not often my area of expertise.

I am prepared to give you some things coming down the timeline, that you will be able to look back upon, and verify my predictions retrospectively.

The Stock Markets will soon complete their controlled demolition. After an initial 'appearance' that the 'bail outs' and 'rescue packages' have steadied the ship, there will be new record lows by the end of the month.

Our Financial Institutions will later call in all loans. There will be many bankruptcies and foreclosures.

The only way John McCain will become the next US President, will be if something "happens" to Barack Obama before the election. If there even is an election. If a certain faction get their way, there will not be. Remember, **behind the scenes, there is only One Party. Our Party**. 'Democracy' is an illusion which is created to uphold your slavery. Whichever side 'wins'; the Family wins. There are many possibilities and alternative 'scripts'. All of them lead toward the ultimate implementation of the overall blueprint of our Creator.

Unless any unforeseen disruptions delay it's announcement, there will be a **new currency by the end of 2008 / early 2009, along with a new Union of nations. January has been spoken of in some circles, as the latest**, though there are plans underway which could even bring this to fruition much earlier than initially hoped for. It **depends upon the results of other upcoming events as to how this will play out**. I am not high enough up the Hierarchy to know the intimate details of the dates and times that far in advance. There is a 'tree system' in which such knowledge is passed down, as and when it becomes 'need to know'. I would be considered to be a "Regional" leader. Above me, are National and International.

San Francisco and Damascus, will be uninhabitable by the end of 2010, possibly even sooner. Again, it depends upon certain 'forces' at play, and which timelines are activated. Humanity, though utterly unconscious of the fact, has a significant part to play in this. You (as a collective consciousness of the planet) are choosing the Negative Polarization by default, by the quality of your thoughts and actions. **Thought is creative energy, focused. You get exactly what you put out**.

Why do you think the Media is so important to us? You have (as a society), in your hypnotized comatose state, given your Free Will consent to the state your planet is in today. You saturate your minds with the unhealthy dishes served up for you on your televisions that you are addicted to, violence, pornography, greed, hatred, selfishness, incessant 'bad news', fear and 'terror'. When was the last time you stopped, to think of something beautiful and pure? **The planet is the way it is, because of your collective thoughts about it**. You are complicit in your inaction, every time you 'look the other way' when you see an injustice. Your 'thought' at the sub-conscious level of creation to the Creator, is your allowance of these things to occur. In so doing, you are serving our purpose. **It is very important to us, that the Polarization of this planet is Negative at the time of the Great Harvest. That means Service to Self orientated, as opposed to Positive, Service to Others. We require a Negative Harvest, and you are doing a fine job of helping us to attain our goal. We are very grateful.**

There will be d**ramatic changes to your climate and weather conditions** over the next few years, as the time of the Great Harvest approaches. You will see windspeeds surpassing 300 miles per hour at times. There will be raging tsunamis and widespread devastation; and a solar emission in late 2009 early 2010 that will cause major melting of the ice caps, and subsequent drastic rise in sea levels, leaving many (international) metropolitan areas underwater.

That is all I have time for at present. I have a Sacrifice I must attend now.

No, not really.

Let's see if we can increase the 'depth' of enquiry and question matter in the next session. Seek beyond the superficial. Get to the 'Core' of the matter.

[End of End of first session]

Click here to read the follow-up discussions by members of the "Above Top Secret Forum".

Second Session:

ATS: How do you know that your bloodline deserves to lead and the rest deserve to follow? Wealth and power is self-propagating therefore I say to you that your bloodline only comprises the 'extreme elite' of the world because your ancestors came to power by chance in the beginning, not because your kind are special. In fact, there's nothing special, clever or honourable in enslaving others.

HH: It is not about 'deserving' or not. Does one 'deserve' to be born English, or American, or Italian, or French, or German, and so on? We came not to power by 'chance', but rather, (which I know may be hard to swallow) by intelligent design. This path of ours was not 'chosen' by us, but rather it was appointed, and accepted.

ATS: Who is your "creator" and is your "creator" the same as our "creator"?

HH: This is an excellent question, which I can use to draw our communication closer to the 'Core'.

Yes and no. You would first need to understand the Creation.

In the Beginning, there is The Infinite One. This is the Source of All. Intelligent Infinity. It is the undifferentiated absolute. Within It, is unlimited potential, waiting to 'become'. Think of it as the "uncarved block" of your Taoist traditions.

Infinite Intelligence, becoming 'aware' of Itself, seeks to experience Itself, and The One Infinite Creator is 'born', or 'manifest' (This appears to your 3rd Density comprehension as "Space"). In effect, the 'Creator', is a point of focused Infinite Consciousness or awareness, into Infinite Intelligent Energy. The One Infinite Creator also becoming self aware, seeks too to experience Itself as Creator, and in so doing, begins the next step down in the Creational spiral. The One Infinite Creator, in focusing It's Infinite Intelligence, becomes Intelligent Energy (which you could call **the Great Central Sun**), and divides Itself into smaller portions of Itself, that can then in turn experience themselves as Creators (or Central Suns). In other words, **each Central Sun (or Creator) is a 'step down' in Conscious awareness (or distortion) from the Original 'thought' of Creation. So "In the beginning" was not "The Word", but Thought**. The Word, is thought expressed and made manifest as Creator.

There is Unity. **Unity is All there is. Infinite Intelligence, and Infinite Energy. The two are One**, and within them, is the potential for all Creation. This state of Consciousness could be termed as 'Being'.

Infinite Intelligence does not recognize it's 'potential'. It is the undifferentiated absolute. But **Infinite Energy recognizes the potential of 'becoming' all things, in order to bring any desired experience into 'being'.**

Intelligent Infinity can be likened to the central 'Heartbeat' of Life, and Infinite Energy as the Spiritual 'Life-blood' (or potential) which 'pumps out' for the Creator to form the Creation.

This image may assist your comprehension:

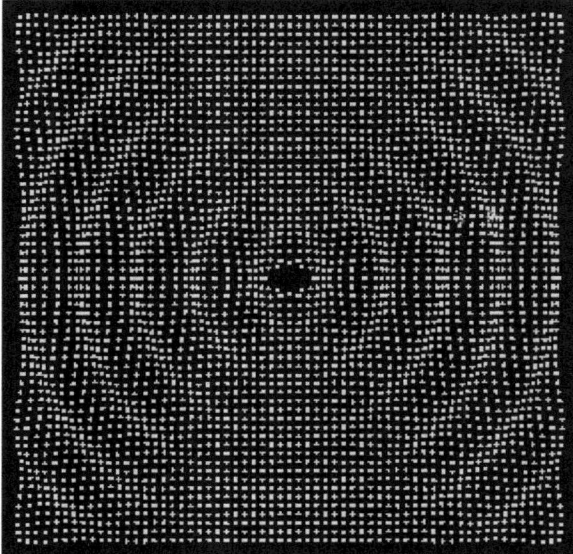

Creation is based upon the **'Three Primary Distortions of The Infinite One'**.

1). Free Will:

In the first Law (or distortion) of Creation, the Creator receives the Free Will to know and experience Itself as an individuated though (paradoxically) unified aspect of The One.

2). Love:

In the second Law of Creation, the initial distortion of Free Will, becomes a focus point of awareness known as Logos, or 'Love' (or The Word in biblical terms). Love, or Logos, using It's Infinite Intelligent Energy, then takes on the role of co-creating a vast array of physical illusions ('thought forms') or **Densities (which some call Dimensions)** in which according to It's Intelligent design, will best offer the range of 'potential' experiences in which It can know Itself.

In effect, the One Infinite Creator, in dividing Itself into Logos, could be termed in your 3rd Density understanding as a **'Universal Creator'**. In other words, Logos, creates on a Universal level of Being. Logos creates physical Universes, in which It and the Creator may experience theirself.

("Let there be Light")

3). Light:

To manifest this Infinite spiritual or 'Life-Force' Energy into a physical thought form of Densities, Logos creates the third distortion, of Light. From the three original Primary distortions of The One into making the Creation, arise myriad hierarchies of other sub-distortions, containing their own specific paradoxes. The goal of the Game is to enter into these in further divions of Creation, and then seek to harmonize the Polarities, in order to once again know Oneself as the Creator of them.

The nature of all such physically manifest Energy, is Light. Wherever thus exists any form of physical 'matter', there is Light, or Divine Intelligent Energy at it's Core or Centre.

Something which is Infinite cannot be 'other than', or 'many', **An Infinite Creator knows only Unity**. Thus, drawing upon It's Infinite Intelligence, the Infinite Creator designed a blueprint based on the finite principles of **Free Will of Awareness**

and sub-level Creations, which in turn, could become aware of themselves, and seek to experience themselves as Creators. And so the "Russian Doll" style experiment was 'stepped down' and down and down. Levels of Creation within levels of Creation.

The One Infinite Creator (or Great Central Sun) steps down It's Infinite Energy to become Logos. Logos in turn designs vast Universes of Space (as yet unmaterialized), stepping down and splitting Itself again, into Logoi (plural), in other words, into an array of Central Suns which will each become a Logos (or 'co-creator') of It's own Universe, with each unique individualized portion of the One Infinite Creator, containing within It as It's very essence, Intelligent Infinity.

Using the Law of Free Will, each Universal Logos (Central Sun) designs and creates It's own version or perspective of 'physical reality' in which to experience Itself as Creator. Stepping down again, It focuses It's Intelligent Energy and creates the unmanifest form of Galaxies within Itself, and splits Itself into yet further 'co-creator' portions ('Sub-Logos' or Suns) which in turn will then design and manifest their own ideas of physical reality in the form of points of Conscious Awareness that we call Suns Stars and Planets.

A 'planetary entity' (or 'Soul') begins the first Density of experience, into which another individualized portion of The One can incarnate. **Just as with all Logos and Sub Logos of Creation, each Soul is yet another smaller unique portion of The Infinite One.** At first, the Intelligent Energy of the planet is in a state that you could call 'chaos', meaning that It's Energy is undefined. Then the process begins again. The planetary Energy begins to become aware of Itself (**the 1st Density of awareness is 'Consciousness'**), and the Planetary Logos (sub-sub-Logos in effect) begins to create other downward steps within Itself, and the internal make up of the planet begins to form; as the raw elements of air and fire combine to 'work on' the Waters and Earth, thus arising conscious awareness of their 'being', and the process of 'evolution' begins, forming the 2nd Density.

2nd Density beings begin to become aware of themselves, as being 'separate', and thus begin to evolve toward the **3rd Density of self-conscious-awareness, (the lowest Density into which a 'human soul' can incarnate).**

Humans in turn (or the Souls incarnated within them), seek to 'return to the Light' and Love, from which they came, as they begin the journey of progression, from 3rd Density up to the 8th Density, and the return to The Infinite One-ness.

Explanation of the Densities beyond 'normal' human consciousness is another question though, so if you wish to know more about them, someone will need to ask an intelligent question which I can respond to, so as not to impinge upon your Free Will not to know.

So, having set forth the above, I can return to further elucidate on your original question:

ATS: Who is your "creator" and is your "creator" the same as our "creator"?

HH: As I said, yes, and no. Ultimately, every living thing (and all things are living) is created by the One Infinite Creator's initial Universal Creation. So yes, taken from that perspective, The One Infinite Creator focuses It's Infinite Intelligence into an awareness point of Infinite Energy, and brings the whole of Creation into Being, though, **we are not directly created by the One Infinite Creator, but rather by our own Logos', Sub-Logos, and Sub-Sub-Logos and so on.** So from that perspective, whilst we are all essentially 'made up' of the same 'stuff' of Creation, initiated by the One Infinite Creator, our actual personal Creators are different portions or Sub-Logos of The One. In other words, yes, our Creator, whilst originating from the same Source, is not the same entity as your Creator.

Which brings me on to a question from another poster (I will continue with your other questions afterwards, but this enables me to indirectly answer the first aspect of your question without having to ask you to rephrase it, due to having to carefully dance around the Free Will issues).

ATS: You say that you come from 13 origonal blood lines. Yet the dna mapping project clearly proved that all humanity desends from only 3. Does this mean you arent human?

HH: An excellent question, thank you. Yes, that is correct, in a manner of speaking. **If you were to meet me walking down the street, I would appear just as human as you do.** We've been incarnating here with you for generations, yet, our bloodlines do not originate from this planet.

ATS: Your answer to the 6 displines of learning are quite similiar to a book about **atlantis** that was supposed to have been channeled, was this also a time for your bloodlines to post answers?

HH: Yes, that is correct, again, in a manner of speaking. **Other, shall we say "off world entities" also visited the planet at that time, and passed down their own understandings of Creation as well as their 'technology',** from what we could best describe as being 'a future aspect of yourselves'. It was Humanity's errors in handling this information that ultimately led to the destruction of Atlantis.

Having now answered a question on whether or not our lineage is of Human origin, I can return to tie in that answer with an explanation as to "Who is our Creator". I'm dancing close to the line in answering this, but the record needs to be set straight, and I should just about be able to get away with it without incurring my own 'upline's' displeasure.

Let us get to the crux of the matter.

Your Creator, the one you have called 'Yahweh', is not "God" inasmuch as your bible refers to him as being "the One True God". He is 'a' Creator (or Sub-Sub-Logos) rather than the One Infinite Creator. He is not even a Galactic level Logos, but rather, is **the Planetary Logos for this one planet**.

Our Creator, is the one you refer to as 'Lucifer', "The Light Bearer" and "Bright and Morning Star".

Our Creator is **not "The Devil"** as he has been spuriously portrayed in your bible. Lucifer is what you would call a **"Group Soul" or "Social Memory Complex",** which has evolved to the level of the Sixth Density, which in effect, means that he (or more accurately '"we"') has evolved to a level sufficient that he (we) has attained a **status equal or arguably 'greater' than that of Yahweh (we have evolved higher than him)**. In appearance, were you to gaze upon Lucifer's fullest expression of our Being, the appearance would be that of a Sun or a "Bright Star". Or, when stepping down into a 3rd Density vibration, we would appear as what you may term an 'Angel' or 'Light Being'.

Allow me to elucidate:

When an entity (Group Soul Complex) evolves to the level of the Sixth Density, it is by comparison to the amount of time it takes to get that far, a mere hop skip and a jump from 8th Density Ultimate Re-Union with The One Infinite Creator, and then from there, **back to dissolution into the Source of All, Intelligent Infinity.**

We (our Bloodline Families), as a Group Soul or Social Memory Complex (Lucifer), were on the verge of Seventh Density Ascension, though at this level, before Harvest comes, we have the choice to progress higher, or, to return to help others of lower densities with their own evolution, by passing down our knowledge and Wisdom (Light) to those that call upon us for assistance, with their own Free Will.

Now, at this time, having made our decision to stay and help our Galactic Brothers and Sisters in The One, **we were assigned a challenging task by the Council of Elders, who act as the Guardians of this Galaxy from their Eighth Density 'Head Quarters' on the planet Saturn.**

Yahweh, due to the fact that he had NOT (as was his right as Planetary Logos) handed down his own Free Will to "know thyself" to those incarnating upon 'his' planet, was having very little evolutionary progress therein. So we (Lucifer) were sent to help. Once the order was given from the Council of Elders, **we "Fell", or Descended back to a place where we could, with hard work and focus, once again materialize a 3rd Density manifestation of ourself.**

Yahweh had agreed to our coming, in fact it was he who had initially asked the Council for a "Catalyst" of change to enter into his Creation, and share the knowledge and wisdom we had attained through our Ascensions. In the absence of Free Will upon the planet, there can be no Polarity, and therefore, nothing to 'choose' between. Just as is portrayed in the book of Genesis, **the planet was very "Edenic" in nature.** Sure, it was a lovely 'paradise', yet the Beings incarnating there had no agitator toward evolving beyond the 3rd Density, and therefore, little hope of ever making the journey Home, to The One. Yahweh has been happy to keep his own little pet Eden Project in effect, but with little chance of the Souls here making it Home, it had become in effect, an albeit very beautiful 'Prison'. Yahweh was, in modern parlance, running a benign dictatorship.

......

Without Polarity, (derived from Free Will), there is only the Unity of Love and Light, and no choice to experience 'other than' that. So, we were to be the Catalyst for change, in order to provide that choice, thus bringing Polarity. Yahweh agreed that we would introduce the concept of Free Will to Earth's inhabitants, by offering them an initial choice, as to whether they 'wanted' it or not. Hence, **"The Tree of the Knowledge of 'Good and Evil'"** (or more accurately, the Knowledge of Polarity, of Positive or Negative). Yahweh takes his inhabitants to a new 'garden' and tells them you can do anything you like, except this one thing, thus creating the desire to do the one thing there are told they cannot. Hence, a "Choice". We provide the Catalyst by telling them the benefits of attaining Knowledge, they eat from the tree, and the rest is history.

Yahweh thought that his 'Children' would still choose to obey him, and when he discovered they did not, he became angry. As he himself describes in his scriptures, he is a "Jealous God", and he did not like it that his 'children' had chose to disobey him, and follow our advice. We're already committed to being here for a predefined set of "Cycles" to help provide the Catalyst for Human evolution, namely by offering you the Negative Option, or that which you choose to call "evil". Now that Free Will had been granted, Yahweh could not retract it, and we have to stay here as contracted to continue to provide the planet with the Polarity choice. Since then, Yahweh has confined us (as a Group Soul) here within the Earth's Astral Planes (which is very constricting and uncomfortable for a Being of our Wisdom and experience). The Council of Elders gave us the choice to be released (against Yahweh's will), but at the cancellation of our contract to Serve the planet earth; or to remain and fulfil our assignment, and endure Yahweh's self proclaimed "Wrath". We stayed, but as a karmic result of our Group Soul's confinement by Yahweh, our own individuated Souls were given the mandate (by The Council) to "Rule" over Yahweh's people during our physical incarnations here on your planet.

Let's be clear about one thing though. All of this (physical life / incarnation), is a very intricate and skillfully designed Game, whereby **the One Infinite Creator, plays the game of forgetting who It is, so that It can learn to remember**, and in doing so, experience and know Itself as Creator. All the way down to us tiny individuated sparks of the All That Is. Off stage, and **between "Lives" (zero-point time / anti-matter Universe)** as incarnated "human beings", we, all of us / you (as Souls), are great friends. Brothers and Sisters in The One.

Between 'lives' we all have a great laugh about the parts we have performed in the 'play', and look forward to and have great fun preparing the next chapters to act out.

I hope that during the above answer, I have also adequately covered your question on "what is our interpretation of good vrs evil? If not, please say, and I will go into more detail.

ATS: Can you elaborate on the "coming harvest" and what exactly you mean by harvest?

HH: I can. I will combine my answer to you with my reply to the following question:

ATS: Is 2012 harvest time? When you speak of the harvest, it has echoes of Chaos Gnosticism in the sense that we are divine souls trapped in the physical world, continuously re-incarnated into flesh until the time that we reach such a level of spiritual 'gnosis' that we are able to avoid being re-incarnated in our next cycle. Is this the foundation of your belief?

HH: Another excellent (and very insightful) question. Thank you.

The higher the quality of the question, the more depth I can give to my answer. It all has to do with the Laws of Confusion and Free Will.

Yes, the noonday Winter Solstice Sun of December 21st, 2012 is the time when the Lord of The Harvest shall return. **You might know him as "Nibiru".**

Read up on the Mayan Prophesies and Calendrical events for more detail upon how the actual Galactic and Universal Cycles work. The "Travelers" who gave them this information were the same ones who visited the the Civilization of Atlantis. The Mayans used that information by creating with the Positive vibration of the Polarity. The Atlanteans opted for the Negative.

Yes, to answer your question. There is much truth in some of the ancient Gnostic texts, though there are also distortions. The information is not 'pure'. It came through many 'filters'.

You are indeed what you call "Divine Souls"; you are sparks or seeds of The One Infinite Creator. You are Life Itself (Light), remembering and learning who you really are (we came here to help you to do this) and yes, currently, you are trapped (or more accurately "Quarantined") within the 'matter' of this planet you call Earth.

You can thank your Creator Yahweh for that. You are the 'offspring' or individuations of his Group Soul (or Social Memory Complex). **Macrocosmically speaking, you ARE Yahweh. The 'Karmic' effect of his imprisoning us in his Astral Planes, also has an impact upon you.** I cannot be more specific on this, without impinging on the Law of Confusion. You must work it out for yourselves.

As for the question of can I elaborate on the coming Harvest, yes, I shall do so now.

Your planet abides by the laws of the Creation of your Galactic Logos. The Galaxy runs on Cycles of time, known as the Precession of the Equinoxes. As I said, **seek the Mayan Calendar for a deeper insight as to how the Galaxy runs (it is highly accurate)**, but for the purpose of this discourse, I will give a brief overview.

The Maya use an astrological cycle called the "Precession of the Equinoxes". This is a 26,000 year cycle in which Earth transits through each of the 12 signs of the zodiac for about 2,152 years each. Each of these astrological ages represents one month of the grand Cosmic Year. This "Mayan" cycle also corresponds to a 26,000 year relationship of the Sun (Solar Logos) orbiting Alcyone, the central star of our Seven Sisters Pleiades constellation.

The End of this Cycle, heralds literally, a New World Age, and a New Creation. "A new Heaven, and a new Earth", and is the time of the Great Harvest.

Smaller Cycles yield a Harvest, and then life continues on the planet as normal. Great Cycles yield a Great Harvest, and the end of current life on the 3rd Density. See it as a kind of 'Cosmic jet wash' and deep clean, while the planet takes a rest and regenerates herself..

When this Life-Cycle Ends, "All things will pass away, and All things shall be made new".

Collectively, Humanity right now, is growing, and developing, into the Beings you have long been encoded to be. Yet, as with any labor, it is not the mother or the baby who is in charge, it is the Primal process of Birth itself, unfolding it's own destiny.

So, **December 21, 2012 AD**, is not the day where all of the sudden the lights go out, and everything will suddenly change, rather, we are NOW in the process of this transition, from one World Age to the next. The changes are underway and will continue steadily accelerating as we head towards the culminating date.

The 26,000 year cycle is composed of 5 lesser cycles, each of which are 5,125 years in duration. Each of these 5 cycles is considered its own World Age or Creation Cycle.

Our present great cycle (3113 B.C. - 2012 A.D.) is called the Age of the Fifth Sun.

This fifth age is the synthesis of the previous four. The initial date that Earth entered the Fifth World, was August 13, 3113 BC, written in Mayan long count notation as 13.0.0.0.0.

To help you understand this Notation:

13=Baktuns, 0=Katuns, the 2nd 0=Tuns, 3rd 0=Uinals, 4th 0=Kin

These are the Mayan words for the periods of time:

Day = Kin (pronounced: keen)
Month of 20 days/Kin = Uinal (wee nal)
Year of 360 days/Kin = Tun (toon)
20 Tuns/years = K'atun (k'ah toon)
20 K'atuns = Baktun (bock toon)
a Baktun is 5,125 years

13.0.0.0.0.

Every day from that point is reckoned by the number of days passed since the event of this cosmic beginning point. **Within the 5,125 year cycle lies 13 smaller cycles, known as the "13 Baktun Count," or the "long count."** Each baktun cycle lasts for 394 years, or 144,000 days. Each baktun was its own Historical Age, within the Great Creation Cycle, with a specific destiny for the evolution of those who incarnated in each baktun.

Planet Earth and her inhabitants are currently traveling through the 13th baktun cycle, the final period of 1618-2012 AD. This cycle is known both as "the triumph of materialism", and "the transformation of matter."

On 13.0.0.0.0, the December solstice sun will be found in the band of the Milky Way, directly in the position of the "Dark Rift" in the Galaxy, forming an alignment between the Galactic Plane and the Solstice Meridian. We are about to enter into a literal alignment of the Cosmic, Galactic, Solar, and Lunar Planes. This is an event that has slowly converged, over a period of thousands of years, and is caused by the precession of the equinoxes. Kind of like a "turning" of the Universal Gears. It brings about the Great Harvest, and the return of the Lord of The Harvest.

"Hidden hand" posted this image to depict "Harvest"

And the planet will complete it's Ascension to the Fourth Density, the vibrational Density of Love. During this Ascension, **there will be a three way split for those Souls inhabiting Earth. Those of the predominantly Negative Polarity, will accompany us as we Graduate through the Negative (or Service to Self) Harvest. We (Lucifer) will Create a new 4th Density Earth, based on the Negative Self Service Polarity. We must 'work off' our own part of the Negative Karmic effect incurred from all the Negativity created on this planet.** Once we have done so, we will be released to once again assume our place as Sixth Density Guardians and Teachers of Wisdom throughout the Galaxy.

Those of the predominantly Positive Polarity (Love and Light) will Ascend to a beautiful new 4th Density Earth, where you will begin to work upon your learning and demonstrating of Love and Compassion. It will be a very beautiful and **"Golden" Age**. The 4th Density begins to open you up to your True Powers as a unique individualized aspect of The One Infinite Creator. **You will perform works and wonders of the like that the one you call "Jesus" promised you would do "and even greater things than these".** It will be a very magical time for you.

For the majority of Humans on the earth who could be considered shall we say "luke warm", they will experience a period of (what will feel 'ecstatic') zero-point time, where you feel totally at One with The Creator, giving you an encouraging reminder and glimpse of who you really are, before the veil of forgetfulness once again descends upon you, and you will be transported to another 3rd Density planet (a kind of 'Earth Replica'), to continue working upon yourselves and learning that life here is all about making choices. You will remain "quarantined" incarnating in 3rd Density matter until the time of the next Harvest; in which time you will need to have proved yourselves that you have learned how to be more Positive Beings, **focused more upon being of Service to others, rather than seeking only to Serve yourself.** When you can do this, and the next Harvest comes, you will have earned the right to join us, and enjoy your inheritance, as a member of the Galactic Community, and you will sit with us as Brothers and Sisters of The One, around the table of our Galactic Governing Body, the Confederation of Planets.

Well, I have imparted much during this session, with thanks to the quality of your enquiries, and I must now take my leave for today.

If you have further questions on the Harvest you wish me to speak in more detail on, if you ask, I can answer. Or any other questions you have too on other matters, I will get to them all as time allows, as with the other (respectfully asked) questions here since I took these away with me to reply to earlier.

If time permits, I will check in with you tomorrow.

ATS: A lot of what you write seems reminiscent of The Ra Material, especially the concept of harvest, STS and STO choices, and intelligent infinity. (More information found here www.llresearch.org...) Have you read that?

HH: It is indeed extremely similar. We both originate from the Source of the Infinite Creator, and we both remember where we come from. I would expect our messages to contain the same Core Truths.

The messages of the **Sixth Density Soul Group 'Ra' is the most accurate information in your mainstream circulation at this point in time**. It is approximately **85-90% accurate**, from what I have seen. The material was brought to my attention when it first came out, something like about 25 years or so ago, if memory serves. I read a lot of it, but not all. I do not have very much free time for that kind of thing, with my many duties. Though others of the Family gave it a close scrutiny to judge it's accuracy, and were very pleased with the end product.

Ra, in fact, is the group I earlier termed 'off world entities' of which visited the Mayan and Atlantean Civilizations. We are acquainted, and friends. Both our Group Soul's are at a very similar level of development / evolution. Both Sixth Density, nearly Seventh. But like us, Ra also chose the path of Service to our fellow Galactic Brothers and Sisters (you, and others), instead of further progression Home. We would recommend that material for any who truly seek understanding. Though, as I said, it is not 100% accurate, so take what resonates.

ATS: What function, if any, do alien abductions have? Why are abductees chosen?

HH: That depends, upon who is doing the "abducting". **Most of what you hear termed as "abductions", are conducted by your own 'governments'. Especially the ones where the 'so-called' "Greys" are involved**. Other than that, sometimes the Confederation will meet with certain incarnates here who have a part to play in "awakening" others to the coming Harvest. These will always be positive experiences, and those who have them will feel uplifted and inspired by their contact.

Then there is the **Orion Empire Group**. Their purposes in visiting you are more along the **Negative** lines. They mainly **target** the ones you have called "**Lightworkers**". They try to put them off their assignments and try to spread fear. They will not actually 'harm' you physically. Mainly their **modus operandi is to restrict you, and deflect you from your path**. They often engage in **psychic attacks that the 'Lightworker' is unaware of, but it does often drain away much of their energy, and make them lack motivation**.

ATS: Why do you want a negative harvest?

HH: It is complicated to put into words, and also I must be careful with what I say on this. I've already had a "slap on the wrist", you could say.

If we do not have a Negative Harvest, we are bound with you for another cycle. Once this Great Harvest is completed, our Contract with the Council and our Creator is also completed. In other words, we have done our duty, and would be free to return to our Fullest Expression, that of Sixth (nearly Seventh) Density Galactic Guardians, and ones who joyfully offer ourselves in Service to the One Infinite Creator, and to our Brothers and Sisters across the Galaxy. However, there is a problem. Well, you would call it a "problem", we call it a Challenge. I will address this later in more detail, in response to another question, but in short, **we need a very high percentage of Negative Polarity, if we are to achieve a Negative Harvest. In other words, we have to be Self-Service-Centred to an extreme**

degree, **in order to become Negatively Harvested**. This is why we work so hard to be as Negatively Polarized as we possibly can be, **If we do not make a high enough percentage, we will miss out, and will end up with the majority "luke warm" percentage, that have to go through another Cycle in 3rd Density**.

By attaining a Negative Harvest, we can still "Graduate" to 4th Density, only it will be a Negative Polarity planet. Not a great place to be. But, as I've stated previously, we (as a Group Soul) have incurred the natural Karmic restitution process that we must work off, for all the Negativity we have caused upon this planet. We will do this for a Cycle in our new 4th Density world, and then we will be freed to once again be the Glorious Being of Light that we truly are. We need a Negative Harvest, so that we can create our 4th Density Earth, and clear our Karmic Record.

Understand, that we HAVE to be Negative. That's what we were sent here to be. It is our contract, and it has always been to help you, by providing the "Catalyst" I spoke of earlier. Being Negative is very hard for us, not on a physical level, (the characters we play enjoy our roles, as we're programmed that way), but on a Spiritual level, it is hard. We surpassed the lowly negative vibrations eons ago. We are Light, and we are Love. It is a very hard thing for us to do Spiritually, to create all this Negativity, but **we do it because we love you, and it is for your highest good, ultimately**. You could say, that it is our Sacrifice that we have made, in order to be of Service to the One Infinite Creator, and to you, our Brothers and Sisters in the One.

Remember, we are all just acting out a grand old game here, where we agree to forget who we really are, that in the remembering, that we may find each other again, and know that we are One. That All of Life, is One.

ATS: I must correct you here. The precession of the equinoxes cannot cause this. It cannot cause anything other than the way in which we here on Earth view the cosmos around us. It concerns the wobble of the Earth's axis and as far as I know does not relate to any other planetary bodies.

HH: From a 3rd Density perspective, you are correct, it "appears" that way. We do not look from a 3rd Density perspective. There is a 'bigger picture' at work that you cannot see.

ATS: Regarding our enslavement, you seem to be saying - essentially - that as fractions of our Logos Yahweh, we are equally responsible for his decision to keep us trapped here on our 3rd density planet Earth. That's an interesting thought. In that sense our total freedom must arrive through a collaborative spiritual effort.

HH: From a certain perspective, what you say is correct. From a 3rd Density view, you see yourselves as being "separate" from everything. From a higher perspective, you see that is not at all the case. **You and your Creator, are One**. As to your statement on your 'total freedom', you are not responsible for those around you. You and they are all One too, when seen from a higher Density, but in this Density, you are here to work upon yourself. You are here to remember who you are, and why you are here. You are here to remember the Infinite Creator. To know your Creator within you, and to offer your Service to him, and others, of your own Free Will choice to Serve. The one comes before the other. **When you remember who you are, and you know it, deep within the Core of your Being, you will know and recognize your 'invisible' connection to All that Is, and in so doing, Joy, and Thanksgiving, and Service, will be the natural outpouring result, from your grateful heart. When you work upon yourself, and learn to know the Creator within you, being of Service to Others will be natural for you, and your Glorious Harvest shall await**.

ATS: One thing I don't get - and perhaps you can explain this to me Hidden-Hand - is why those who belong to Lucifer (and Lucifer himself) do not fight for the freedom of all souls? If Lucifer represents liberty, freedom of will and knowledge, why do those who serve him not do as the Biblical Lucifer did and rebel against the tyranny of the Elders?

HH: This is a very good question, thank you. I will split it into two parts, and answer the second part after this. Firstly, the **Council of Elders** are the absolute opposite of tyrannical. They are the **Wise and Loving Guardians of our Galaxy**. There is so much that one cannot understand from only a 3rd Density perspective. When you reach higher Densities, you see that ultimately, everything balances, and there is only Unity. **All else than Unity, is Illusion, or 'thought-form'**.

The Council gave us a set of choices. We chose to stay here to help you, despite the cost to ourself. That is the nature of Loving Service to Others. The ultimate paradox in all this, is that in this storyline we are all co-creating together, in order for us to be of the most Service to you, we must be utterly self serving. I do so love our Creator's sense of irony.

As to the first part of your question, the biblical depiction of "War in Heaven" is not entirely inaccurate. I shall explain. Our initial contract, was to introduce the Catalyst for Free Will on this planet. When **Yahweh** initially began discourse with the Council of Elders, he was not initially looking for help with introducing Free Will, but rather for guidance on how he could best speed up his (and his inhabitant's) evolutionary process. As I mentioned, he **was running a benign dictatorship**. We had at that time, just completed an assignment in Tau Ceti, and had reported for our next duties. We (as Group Soul Lucifer) were sent on a "fact finding expedition" as it were, to visit Earth, and meet with Yahweh, to evaluate his planetary Creation Laws, and make suggestions on how best he could help his "offspring" (this is the term I shall use to describe the Souls who comprise the Group Soul) and thusly Yahweh, to progress.

We explored many options, and reported our findings to the Council, and to Yahweh. It was our best evaluation, that the **only real and fast track way to increase his evolvement meaningfully, was the introduction of Free Will**. It was not specifically the implementation of Free Will that Yahweh wanted help with, it was simply **the introduction of a Catalyst**. He was not at all pleased with our report that he needed to implement Free Will. He was happy with his little pet paradise, and he didn't want to "loose control" of it. In the end the Council persuaded him that it was the best way, and he reluctantly agreed. We returned to Earth, and had a cordial meeting with Yahweh, discussing how we could best implement the Free Will option. Yahweh was adamant that his offspring would choose to be loyal to him anyway, and that they were so contented with their way of life, that they would always trust him and do as he said was best. That, he said, was his "main reason" that Free Will would not work well as the Catalyst. That's why he agreed to the experiment of the Tree of Knowledge. He believed it would prove him "right". When it did not, he became angry, threw his toys out of the pram, and his offspring out of the garden, and laid a big guilt trip on them about how they had broken his trust and disobeyed him. That's not really an Honourable way for a Logos to behave, but hey, that's the beauty of Free Will I guess.

Next "problem" to occur, was that his offspring were so grateful to us for our help, that Yahweh became (in his own admission) a "**Jealous God**". Then we had the whole "you shall have no other gods than me" thing. We were not pleased with the situation at all, as a Logos should not be behaving like this with his offspring, they are One, after all. When we attempted to leave the planet to return to the Council, Yahweh prevented our departure. We tried to leave again, and were then thrown down into the Astral Planes and confined therein. The Council ordered us to be released, but said **we would have to cancel our contract to help the Souls on Earth to evolve**. We didn't want to leave, we found them very likable Beings, really Positively Polarized, and we wanted to stay and help, we just wanted also to be free to come and go as we pleased. The only way we could stay, was to stay confined as a Group Soul, which meant **Cycles of incarnation for us** (as individuated Souls), which we had not done for a long while. As I've stated before, there is no 'wrong' or 'right' seen from a Higher Density, but there are still consequences for every action. Such is the **law of Karmic effect**. The contract had already been made between Yahweh, us, and the Council for us to provide the Catalyst so we had a right to be there, the Karmic effect of Yahweh imprisoning us on the Macrocosmic level, was that his individuated Souls would be imprisoned on the microcosmic level. The Infinite Creator gave Yahweh (and all) the gift of Free Will to Create as we choose, but the Karmic effect of his choice was the **Council quarantining the planet**. A certain evolutionary level is required to be a functioning part of a Positive Unified Galactic Society.

As for "fighting for the freedom of all souls", remember that ultimately, this is a Game, that we are all playing here. We are actors, playing on the "stage of Life". This 'world' is all illusion, or 'though-form'. **No one really "dies", and no one is really hurt. In between incarnations, you know this very well**. But the rules of the game ensure that you must forget who you really are, so that you believe it is all 'real' whilst you are playing the game of Life. That is an essential prerequisite when you are making choices. Otherwise, the game would be too easy.

This world is not reality. Though we can express Reality in it, if we so chose.

ATS: OK, so your family and fellow elites might be as entrapped in the Earthly realm as we are, but why actively propagate and aid the forces of enslavement?

HH: Because that is the part we have been contracted to play, in this game. In order to "win" (or more accurately to be successful in) the Game, we must be as Negatively Polarized as possible. Service to Self in the extreme. Violence, War, Hatred, Greed, Control, Enslavement, Genocide, Torture, Moral Degradation, Prostitution, Drugs, all these things and more, they serve our purpose. In the Game. **The difference between us and you, in the Game, is that we know that we are "playing"**. The less you know about the Game, and the less you remember that you're a player, the more "senseless" living becomes. In all these Negative things, we are providing you with tools. But you do not see it. It is not what we do, but how you react to it, that is important. We give you the tools. You have the Free Will choice how you will use them. You have to take responsibility. **There is only One of Us here. Understand that, and you will understand the Game**.

ATS: Something I found extremely interesting is the concept of the Grand Age of Precession being split into five 5,125 year cycles. 3113 B.C., the beginning of the current sub-age was a time of great activity. Is the construction of stone monuments in Western Europe, the Middle-East and Egypt at this time related to the recogniton of this cycle? What was the purpose of Britain's stone circles and Egypt's pyramids? They are more than mere markers of an aeon-change. They must have had some enormous significance. Actually, something I'd most like to know is - Were the builders of these monuments members of the enslaved masses who were trying to understand the nature of existence, or were the builders members of your elite bloodline?

HH: Yes, there is significance in these occurrences, according to the space/time of their happenings. The Group Soul Complex Ra, was the architect of these structures. They were Created from Thought. When one understands and sees that all is Illusion, or Thought, one can "use 'The Force" to manipulate the illusions. All things, seen and unseen, are inter-connected Life-Force Energy. Once you know what the magician knows, it's not magic. It's a 'tool of Creation'.

Thank you for your questions, they were very insightful.

ATS: It is your kind that has ruined the world. Thinking of yourselves are higher then anyone. If i saw you in real life, it wouldn't be pretty.

HH: You lack understanding, not to mention eloquence. To understand "Higher", try thinking 'outside of the box' for a moment. If I am walking along the ground, and you are flying above me in an airplane, does that make you better than me?

No. It just makes you Higher.

ATS: I will see you in hell

HH: Be careful what you wish for. All thoughts and words are Creative.

schiass, thank you for your questions. I believe I have already dealt with many of them in my previous answers this session, though if you feel I've missed anything, please say.

ATS: If "Yahweh" is a positive polarity entity, how is he "wrathful" and "jealous"?

HH: Does Yahweh have Free Will? Would you like to think of yourself as reasonably positive? Can you still be wrathful and jealous at times? Is Yahweh a Macrocosm of you?

ATS: Have there been over time other entities pretending to be "Yahweh"?

HH: On occasions, yes.

ATS: I would like to know how do we choose a service to others (positive) path over a service to self (negative).

Is this statement correct? : "**In order to choose the positive path, at least 51 percent of our thoughts and actions must be dedicated to the service of others. For the negative path, at least 95% must be self-serving. Between the two lies "the sinkhole of indifference".**"

HH: Your statement is correct, yes. So you see, how hard we must strive for negativity? It takes a lot of effort to reach 95% Negativity. Also, you may be surprised how many people on the planet are nowhere near reaching 51% Positive.

ATS: **How do you choose a Service to others path**?

HH: Be good to yourself. Cultivate a genuine Love for Life, and for Being. Be genuinely thankful to the Infinite Creator every day, for bringing you into Being, and for his bountiful provision. You have "survived" this far, have you not? You may not have everything you want, but you have everything you need, in order to complete that which you incarnated here to do. Give thanks for that. Show acknowledgment and gratitude to the Infinite Creator, for all that It has done, and is doing for you. It has given you the gift of Life Experience, and offered you the Free Will to decide what you will Create with it. Guard your thoughts carefully, as they are more powerful than you may imagine. **When you are coming from a place of Love for, and Service to your Creator, a life of Service to others will become a natural outflowing from that.** Always look for ways that you can be of assistance to your fellow Beings. Being of encouragement to others. Build people up, and do not put people down. Be a beacon of light, in a dark world.

Does that old lady need a hand with her shopping bags? How do you treat the homeless man who asks you for some spare change for the shelter? Ever heard about "Angels in disguise"? Look and see the Divine Spark in the Heart of all Beings. Treat them as you would like to be treated yourself, and as you would your Creator if he was speaking directly with you. "For even as you are doing it to the least of these, you are doing it unto me". The Law of Radiation and Attraction. Your thoughts, words, and actions return to you. Ultimately, cultivate a spirit of humble Gratitude. You won't go far wrong with that. Desire to Serve flows naturally from a grateful heart.

ATS: If we live with a "service to others" philosophy in order to achieve oneness with the infinite source, isn't that really "service to self"? How is the distinction of negative and positive polarity made?

HH: You do not Serve others to achieve Oneness with the Infinite Source, you Serve others, because you love them, as yourself. Others, are an extension of yourself. That's why the Law of Attraction works the way it does. **Truly, whatever you are doing to me, you are doing to yourself**. We are All One, in the Infinite Creation. Separation is an illusion, because you only see what is in the 3rd Density. You do not see the whole picture.

We achieve Oneness with the Infinite Source of All, as a result of our upward spiral of progression. We are all on the path back to where we came from. We are All on our way back Home.

ATS: It is my understanding that all souls must eventually choose the positive path to unite with the infinite creator. If this is true, what is the justification of choosing the negative path now, for your people and us?

HH: An astute question. Yes, all Souls eventually learn that Positive is the pathway which leads Home. But whilst incarnating in the 3rd Density, **Negativity is still an important tool in your learning process**. It teaches you "other than". As I said earlier, it is up to you how you use the tools we have given you. **Do you respond to Negativity with more Negativity? Has fighting fire with fire ever worked for you?** Or do you choose to see the Negativity as t**he tool that it is, and recognize that it is offering you an opportunity?** I will honour your Free Will to think and discover for yourself what that opportunity is.

ATS: Or if the one infinite creator is "Love", does that mean it doesn't matter if we choose love of others or love of ourselves? Will either path will lead to the source?

HH: In a sense, you are correct, to a certain point. But there is a **big difference between loving yourself, and being selfish**. A big difference. When you truly understand what it is to Know and Love 'yourself', you cannot help but to Love and Serve others. There are no 'others'. When you understand this, at the Core level of your Being, you will be on the path Home, to the Infinite Creator, and ultimately, submergence back into The Infinite Oneness.

ATS: I agree with many others that your answers are very much in line with several sources I have read in the past, including the channellings of Ra, the Cassiopians and several others.

Can you explain your interpretation of such "channellings" and if they are another source of disclosure from your people?

HH: I have spoken on Ra in my previous answers today. I have not heard of Cassiopians. There are no other communications from my Family at this time, than this one, though there is a possibility of another soon, depending upon certain events.

My general view of "channellings" is that the majority of them are of very poor quality. That is not necessarily a slight against those bringing them through, but more a matter of their lack of receptivity and subsequent distortions. It is very rare, to find a good, stable, clear, and impartial channel. The key element in channeling, is the ability to temporarily withdraw the "filters" of your own personal beliefs and be a clear channel. To bring through what is actually given, not your slant on what you think it might mean. When I am saying 'you', I mean this in a general term of course here, not 'you' personally. Always remember that it's meant to be about the Message, not the messenger. The Ra channellings are very accurate indeed. They are the only ones I know of that I would be happy to classify as a "Clear" message. Though as I say, even then it's not 100%. More like 85-90%.

Another difficult issue with channeling, is that you can start off recieving a Positive entity, and if you are not very perceptive in your discernment and careful in your protection when identifying an incoming channel, you can get a Negative one that pretends to be positive, but gradually slips in more and more misinformation, having gained your trust. **The ones that give you precise dates and times are nearly always ones to avoid. Positive entities will not give a date and time. Negative ones will do, so they can set you up for a fall. Once you're tricked into predicting dates and times, and they don't happen, they've succeeded in putting out the Light of your message, as no one will see any credibility in you.**

ATS: Well, now we know the point of this thread, someone just discovered new age theology and wanted to take the time to type out his discovery.

OP, still waiting for you to provide a prediction with a time line. So far all you've offered is general doom, which is what everyone on ATS predicts every year. Need something SPECIFIC in the NEXT WEEK.

Of course I know you won't provide anything. This is a hoax.

HH: This will be the only time that I reply to you.

At the outset of our discourse here, I made it expressly clear the way I am choosing to operate. If you do not like my choices, you have the Free Will to not read this disclosure. I would kindly suggest that you use it, as your energy is feeling very frustrated and angry. That's not really an advisable direction to want to be heading, under the circumstances.

As I took the time to explain to you before, I have nothing to prove to you. That is not why I came. Believe, or do not believe, I am Divinely indifferent. If my presence here ends up benefiting just one Soul during the process, it will have been worth the effort. I have not asked you to believe, the only thing I have respectfully asked, was that you 'suspend judgment' or hold a 'provisional faith' until the discourse is complete, so that the flow of questions / information remains uninterrupted. You have shown me nothing but discourtesy and bad manners from the outset, and then wonder why I do not respond. If you do not like the topic, simply choose not to read or reply, and let those that do wish to participate with insightful questions do so uninterrupted.

Your points:

1) New age theology? That is amusing. You clearly have not the faintest comprehension of just how ancient and timeless these "mysteries" are. I find it ironic "LowLevelMason", that if you ever make it to the 32nd Degree, you're going to find yourself hearing these Truths all over again. I hope that you will find it easier to integrate these Truths then, and I ask our Infinite Creator to guide your path.

2) You will not be receiving any times or dates from me. I am not here to "Prove" anything, and I have no need to do so. Your disbelief is of no consequence to me. Only to you.

I am here to diligently discharge the duty given to me, of delivering a message. And I will complete that duty regardless of you feelings about it.

3) As to your point regarding "doom and gloom", that just serves to reveal your mindset. Where you see "doom and gloom" I see opportunity. Life conforms to your ideas about the way it is for you. If you see "doom and gloom", then that is what you are projecting. The world is your mirror. It reflects back to you what you are putting out. If you do not like the reflection Life is showing you, then change that which is causing it.

ATS: You see, if this really existed there would be countless thousands of people involved, and any one person could leak.

HH: Thousands? Try Millions. And you have no possible comprehension of the rigorous training and the harshness of the conditioning we undergo from an early age. No one dares to go against the Family. We know what would happen if we did. But that is not the prime motivator. The motivator is unbridled Loyalty to the Family, and our Creator. We understand the importance of what we are doing here, even though most of humanity does not.

ATS: Oopsie, OP. You just shot yourself in the foot. For someone who only deals with manipulating the spiritual side of life you sure do know A LOT about things that have nothing to do with it. You just exposed yourself.

HH: Do you not sit down with your family, and keep one another abreast of your plans?

As to your remarks about my "Spiritual" role, the ignorance you demonstrated is most humorous to us. If you think I 'only' deal in the Spiritual, you have either not read, or misread my posts. You also make the assumption that my role is about "manipulating" the "spiritual side of life". Again, you lack understanding, and then make false judgments about that which you have no comprehension of. You would do well to stop trying to be "clever", and instead channel all this misplaced aggressive energy of yours into something more productive and nourishing for your Soul. But don't let me stop you, you're contributing nicely to the overall Negative Polarity of the coming Harvest. We are Grateful to you.

I will be spending the last few days of my time here (our discourse ends on Friday) focusing on responding to insightful questions with depth, which make the most of this opportunity for sharing information and making connections on a Soul level of Being, so please do not expect any further responses to your verbal jousting, I neither have sufficient time or inclination for engaging in insignificant banter.

To those who's questions I have not yet had time to reply to, I will do so tomorrow. In the meantime while I catch up, I respectfully ask if you will please hold off on further questions until I am up to date with the current ones.

Thank you to those who have contributed to this discourse so far with meaningful questions. For those with an open mind, it is my hope that you get something out of this information.

Third Session:

ATS: Im wondering if you can help me. My name is Shelby David, and I am here for the coming trials and tribulations. I am a part of Quetzalcoatl, or the rebirth of it, as far as I know. I know many of your words to be true because I had already re-discovered these truths through finding that which resonated most with me through the various belief structures of this planet.

HH: Good evening Shelby. It is good to 'see' you again. It has been a while old friend. Would it surprise you to know that we were 'expecting' you?

Quetzalcoatl is also a Sixth Density Group Soul (Social Memory Complex). Some refer to Quetzalcoatl as an "Ascended Master", although he would be most amused by that title, knowing as he does, that 'Mastery' is still some way off at this point for him, as well as it is for ourselves (as **Group Soul Lucifer**). One can be accurately described as having 'Mastered' a particular Density, though Mastery of the entire Creational incarnation Cycle does not occur until one has once again attained submergeance back into the One Infinite Creator. We may choose to do so once attaining 8th Density ascension, or, once may choose instead to progress up to the next Octave of Densities, and begin a new cycle of Creational incarnation challenges.

ATS: This is my first time on earth in a long time, possibly ever. I have known for quite some time and been told by another from one of the bloodlines in your group that I do not truly exist here.

HH: You are correct in that you have not been here for a substantial period of "Earth-Time", though not that you have never been here before. The Group Soul Quetzalcoatl enjoyed many 3rd Density incarnational cycles here back in the Classic Aztec period. He struggled at first with perfecting Love love for others, which held back his progression for some time. However once he had came to the realization of our inherant Unity, he was able to see himself in others, and his (your) progression was rapid from there on in. Your Quetzalcoatl Soul Group attained Positive Harvest with a very impressive 76%, at the time of the subsequent Harvest. Naturally, when a Group Soul is undergoing an incarnational cycle in 3rd Density, It's individualized Soul portions (ie, you) are the ones who are doing the actual physical incarnations, with the "OverSoul" (the "Higher Self") of your individuated Souls acting as the Energy anchor in which the individual Soul sparks are "stepped down" from.

You spent a long while working your way through the **5th Density, the Density of Wisdom, or Light**. This was due in the main part to an over abundance of Compassion (which is not a bad thing, as **Compassion is one of the main things you work on at 4th Density**). However, to Graduate from 5th to 6th Density (the Density of Unity), one must learn the balance between Compassion, and Wisdom. The 6th Density is hence sometimes known as the the Density of Compassionate Wisdom, due to one having learnt the balance between the two. This required many incarnational cycles for you, which is why you correctly feel that you have not visited 3rd Density Earth for a long time.

ATS: I was not expected to show up, I originally had other previous engagements but I managed to get here at the last minute. One of the things I have remembered is that I am too under contract. I am a walk-in, if that makes sense to you, so my human family is not like me. I have spent a long time traveling to various densities and helping in the various revolutions there.

HH: Your insight serves you well Shelby. This not only applies to you, but your entire Soul Group.

Quetzalcoatl (the Macrocosm of yourself) has been busy for the last two cycles working with a 5th Density group on Alpha Centuri, who were experiencing similar problems with an overabundance of Compassion, at the cost [of] personal Wisdom. You recently completed your assignment there, and were eager not to miss out on the glorious opportunity to be a part of this Great Harvest. Whilst your Group as I said, did eventually learn to balance Love / Light to Graduate into the 6th Density Unity vibration, you still are very much prone to extreme compassion, and rather than take the usual period of time/space (**anti-matter universe, where we rest between incarnations**) you were keen to jump aboard this 3rd Density space/time whirlwind at this point, to be of assistance to your fellow Beings here.

ATS: My problem is that my memory has malfunctioned, and some of the things that I have remembered from my previous existences do not correspond with your words. I have met Lucifer and his generals, on more than one occasion. I would appreciate any information you may know of that could clear up my confusion as to why my thoughts are so jumbled, because I know what my path is clearly and I am awaiting the starting point, but I am not completely clear on what truly is happening here. Thank you for your time.

HH: You have indeed 'met' with us (Lucifer) before, on many occasions. We have worked together on various Council and Confederation assignments. Use the gift of your 'Dreamtime' communications (which are important communications from your OverSoul, and many other Sources whereby information is "downloaded") to 'plug in' to your inner data-bank. Begin recording everything you recall upon awaking, and do not give up on the process, even though it is hard at first. You will begin to slowly make sense of the information which is being "downloaded" into your subconscious mind. When you become proficient at this, and can use your 'Dreamtime' as a method of inner communication, ask our Infinte Creator to remind you of your time in the Zeta Reticuli system. You will remember then our last period of Service together, I would hope with much fondness.

Sadly, my time here is only permitted until Friday, therefore we will not likely communicate again after this message. So I wish you the very best with your Assignment here my friend, both your individual one, and that of your Group Soul. I ask that our Infinte Creator bless and guide your path. We look forward to seeing you on 'the other side' when this grand ride is over.

Our Love, Wisdom and Peace be with you.

ATS: You mention Alcyone ... it's interesting there's a celestial map of it at Hoover Dam. There's also a compass, framed by signs of the zodiac.

HH: Indeed. Just like in Hollywood productions. **We hide the Truth right out in the wide open**. What humanity is offered as "Science Fiction", more often than not, is actually Science Fact.

ATS: What do the winged statues, commissioned by the U.S govt, guarding the entrance at the dam really represent? Is any of this collection of celestial symbolism found there connected to your luciferian/alien/equinox/transformation agenda?

HH: That is actually very simple. You'll note that the feet point directly downward to the earth, and the hands and wingtips point directly up to the sky. The Life-Force Energy flows into the human mind/body/soul complex from the earth up through the feet. The Intelligent Energy from the Infinite Creator flows down from above and in through the crown chakra. The wings represent our (Lucifer's) inherent Divinity. You'll also note that the figure is seated. "The seat of our (Lucifer's) Power connects Heaven and Earth, and all things must pass through us".

ATS: Other questions I have, and sorry if you explained this. Are these bloodlines the wealthy, as most assume, or seemingly ordinary people (including celebrities and politicians, etc), blending in with society, going relatively unnoticed, but yet contributing to your cause in the grander scheme of things?

HH: The names you know, have no real power. Sure, they "appear" to have lots of power, in the way earthbound souls perceive power. Our wealth makes the million and billionaire "celebs" and corporate bigwigs look like a child's pocket money. Our wealth is Family wealth, which has passed down through the generations over thousands of years. True wealth however, is knowing deep in your heart, that you and your Infinite Creator, are One. "Seek ye first the Kingdom of 'God' (Infinite Creator), and all these things shall be added unto you".

ATS: So part of this question could also be, are all of them aware they are part of this bloodline, or are some members oblivious to this connection they have? Are they informed of this at a particular age? For example, how and at what age were you told you belonged?

HH: Yes. If you are Bloodline (Family), you are born into it, and you are raised this way, from birth.

There is no other way. **I want to be clear on this Bloodline issue. The ones you know, they are of earthly lineage. Yes, they have their place in the Family, but the Real Power lines, do not originate from this planet.**

ATS: I have probably found this the single most insightful thing so far. It helps me to understand the answers to some of the questions I've asked.

HH: I am glad. It is the probably the singlemost important thing that I have shared.

ATS: Unfortunately, its connotations also alleviate the 'NWO' [def] of most accusations.

HH: That depends upon your perspective. Does it alleviate the Negativity we have perpetuated? No. Does it alleviate the pain and suffering we have caused, and are causing upon the planet? No.

Does it alleviate that we are closing our End Game scenario, and soon to openly come out and offer publically to "save" the failing political and financial institutions with our esteemed Leadership? No.

Does that mean that you should give into and feed the Negativity? No.

Does it alleviate that we will have to spend a Cycle in Karmic restitution, to balance this lifetime of overt Negativity? No.

Does it mean that you should use the Negativity as the tool that it is, to show you that which you are not? Yes.

Remember, always, that this is a beautiful Game that we are playing here and co-creating together, with our Infinite Creator. And that **"off stage" (between lives) we are the very best of friends, and that no one really "dies" and no one really "suffers", except in the Game.** The Game is not Reality. Reality is Reality, and you have the Power to Express your Reality within the Game, once you have learnt how to do so.

ATS: **You are essentially saying that a soul can only choose positivity in a world where negativity also exists. If there were no protagonist in this world, there'd be no opportunity for a human soul to choose 'good' or 'evil' and thus prove on a spiritual level that they deserve one afterlife fate over another. If we only had positivity to choose from, we'd learn nothing and our souls would manage to prove nothing.**

HH: Exactly.

That is the reason why we came. It was a great Sacrifice for us. Hard as it is to comprehend from within the mental confines of 3rd Density life experience, we do it, because we Love you.

ATS: An extremely basic concept but one I'd so far managed to overlook. Unfortunately, for those of us who love our Earthly existence (or rather, the potential it has), it's rather difficult to come to terms with a concept whereby suffering and slavery are as natural as love and happiness and that only after this Earthly existence can we ever be free.

HH: I understand. Our job is to provide the Catalyst. Your's is to use it. Can you look beyond what your eyes are showing you, to find and express Love and Happiness in a world of Fear and Distress? If you can, you will be as a Beacon of Light into the Darkness. **Will you succumb to the Darkness, or will you stand and shine your Divine Inner Light? Only you can make that decision for yourself.**

Think about this:

If the One Infinite Creator, is Infinite, and has created everything that Is (which It is, and It has), then does the Infinite Creator not reside within all things?

When you can see the Divine spark of the Infinite Creator, even within those who would mean you harm, the strong grip of the illusion will begin to lose it's power over you.

"Love your 'enemies', and pray for those who persecute you".

ATS: Thank you Hidden_Hand. Whether you're genuine or not, you've certainly got me thinking and learning.

HH: You are very welcome. I am genuine, but, would it matter even if I were not? Remember, it is not who the messenger is that is of the greatest import, but rather, it is the nature of the Message itself. I wish you well on your journey Home. We will see you on the other side, and we'll all have a good old laugh about the parts we have played in this grand drama.

ATS: Is there any way to cancel this restriction? Because i could be just very lazy or under this kind of spell and want to know wich one it is. Does sleep paralysis have anything to do with it because i get that from time to time with or without shadow figures.

HH: There is. **Research and employ Psychic Shielding techniques**. There is much information on the internet, so I need not spend the little time we have left going into that. Read many sites, and listen to your Inner Voice. Your Soul will guide you if you ask it. It speaks in the language of Feelings. **When it "just feels right", usually, it is**.

No, sleep paralysis is unrelated. That occurs when your brain "awakes" from the dream state before your body. Whilst going through REM deep sleep, it is natural for your body to become paralyzed during the REM cycle, so as to prevent possible injury whilst dreaming. Sometimes when you awake too quickly from a dream, your body just thinks you are still dreaming, and thus the REM paralysis continues for a while, usually until you "shake" yourself awake, often due to the difficulty to breathe.

ATS: And another question. Is it possible that our essence can be destroyed in the coming times or is that just another scare-tactic?

HH: No. Your essence can never be destroyed. You are a unique part of the One Infinite Creator. You are an Eternal Soul, currently residing in a physical shell that you could call an "earth-suit". Your earth-suit will perish, but YOU cannot die. Nothing can destroy the Infinite Creator, and you and the Infinite Creator, are One.

ATS: I go to work to pay my bills, I live a good life with friends, loved ones, people I care about. I am essentially a good person but I do have the full range of emotions as a 'real' human, ie, jealousy, hate etc. I guess I would describe myself as 'luke-warm' to use your phrase.

How can I as an individual take what you say as the 'truth'?

HH: No one is asking you to. Never take what another says to you as "Truth". **Your purpose here, is to find your own Truth**. Sometimes, others can help you to do so by offering guidance, but for their Truth to become your Truth, it must pass through the test of your discernment. Sit quietly in meditation, and ask the Infinite Creator to guide your path. Meditate upon that which I have shared, and listen to your inner feelings. They are the language of your Soul.

Use all your Negative emotions as they arise, as the tools that they truly are. Train yourself to notice when Negativity arises in you. When you catch yourself projecting a Negative thought, remember that all thought is creative, and ask yourself if that is really what you want to create?

It takes a while to become proficient, but do not give up. Just **keep noticing your Negative thought patterns as they arise, and in so doing, simply choose again, and select a response that is more Positive. It is called 'working on yourself', and is the main reason you have chosen to be here right now**. To work upon yourself. I wish you well in your transformation process.

ATS: I also read through the above link from one calling themselves 'The Insider', although his / her posts were less sophisticated than yours. Was he your predecessor? One of your ilk charged with this 'disclosure'?

HH: A good question. I have just read through that material. It was very interesting. No, not a 'predecessor of mine', and not a disclosure I was previously aware of, which had it come from my Family, would be highly strange. Though, I note that he himself stated that he is "from a minority", and certain clues within his writing gives me a very good idea which one.

I would say his material is around 60% accurate. The feelings I get from reading him, are not that he intentionally included inaccurate information, but that he was just not in possession of the "bigger picture". Were he to be from the "minority" group I believe him to be from, that would make perfect sense.

ATS: **So when the Harvest comes, my time here is over and this conscious shell I live in is no more, what then? What happens to me? What happens to my friends and loved ones? Are we, and by we, I mean the vast vast majority of us who possess this planet, this dimension, this density, by and large going to be ignorant of the events you foretell?**

HH: This is a good question. I like questions that come from the heart.

It depends upon the circumstances surrounds your final moments of this particular Lifetime. For example, let us say that the physical aspect of **you was to do the thing called "die" during the coming earth changes, you will immediately return to that wondrous realm in which we reside in between incarnations**, that which we call time/space or 'anti-matter'. **This is the place that humans refer to as "Heaven"**. There you shall meet with all those you love who have also "died" during this life experience, and enjoy a wonderful and emotional reunion. You will **meet up with your Soul Group, and your Spiritual Teachers**. We all store a portion of our Soul Energy on 'the other side' when we come here. Depending upon the difficulty level of the life-experience we've chosen, we take more or less of our Energy with us. **For an average "Lifetime", we typically bring between 60-80% of our Soul Energy into incarnation with us. Therefore, even if ones you love who are already back in the world of Spirit have incarnated again on another adventure, there will still be a part of their Energy there to meet with you, and welcome you Home**. You will then evaluate your life-experience with your Teachers, and learn the lessons of your successes and your mistakes. You will then spend time in learning and resting, before begining to plan your next incarnation.

For those who do not physically "die" before the Great Harvest arrives, there will be a **moment of "zero-point time"**, where you will enjoy an ecstatic merging with the Infinite Creator, giving you a wonderful reminder and reassurance of who and what you really are, before the veil of forgetfulness once again descends upon you, and you will be transported to the place that awaits you, depending upon whether you join us in 4th Density Negative (unlikely), **Graduate to 4th Density Positive (possible)**, or **go to another similar 3rd Density planet (for the "luke-warms") to continue in your learning for however many Cycles it takes you to Graduate to 4th Density Positive.** Those in this category will not remember anything at the time of your transition, it will be just like nothing has changed, except you will retain the memory of your "zero-point" experience to encourage you. You will not remember the recent experiences of the Harvest in this life here. It just be as though you all had some mystical experience, and life will continue as 'normal' for you.

ATS: I find you difficult to believe and yet you respond and inform in a very sophisticated manner, it is quite intriguing.....

HH: That is good. I do not want for you to blindly believe me. Too many on this planet spend their entire lifetime doing and thinking things because others say that they are true.

What I want, is that my words become a Catalyst for you. That is what we came here to do. If my words cause you, even if for just a short time, to stop for a moment, and evaluate that which you 'think' you already know about the nature of Life, and take for granted as being true (because "everyone else believes it"), then my time will have been well spent. My desire is that you become an Authentic Human Being, thinking, and feeling, and deciding for yourself what "feels" like Truth for you. I wish you well in your endeavors.

ATS: You can't provide 1 shred of proof that this isn't a hoax even though it would be incredibly easy to do so, were you who you claim you were.

HH: Won't. Not can't. Big difference.

This is not intended to be an object lesson prophesy fulfillment.

If you think I thought that I would be blindly believed, or even wanted for that to happen, you are very much mistaken. I would be disappointed if that were to be the case, for you will have learned nothing from my time here. (Not you personally, I mean 'you' as in people in general).

My task here, as has been my task incarnating here for thousands of years, is to provide a Catalyst. To make you think. (Again, not 'you' personally, I mean in general).

If I were to give you the "proof" that you are looking for, if I were to predict things and tomorrow they all happen before your very eyes, people would likely take everything I've said here as "gospel". That would be disasterous were that to occur, because you will have learned nothing for yourselves.

It's not about me. I'm just a messenger. It's all about you (again, generally speaking), and what you do in relation to the Catalyst. Question what you "think" you know about reality. Seek the Infinite Creator within you, and ask for It's guidance.

"Ask, and you will receive. Search, and you will find. Knock, and the door will be opened for you".

ATS: I am a 32nd degree Mason, although if you were really a royal bloodline person you would know that it means nothing.

HH: If you have Genuinely attained the level of "Sublime Prince of The Royal Secret" through the Scottish Rite, or that of the "Order of the Knight's Templar" through the York Rite, and have not been taught of the Truths of Creation, then I would be very interested indeed to know which area Lodge you attend, as I would very much like to speak with your current Worshipful Master.

Naturally I completely understand and respect if you do not wish to make such personal details known publicly though.

Of course. what you said in another post about there only being three degrees is true, for those attending the Blue or Craft Lodges, though as you've stated that you are 32nd degree, I'm presuming you are either Scottish Rite, or the York Rite's equivalent.

I hope to be able to be present personally in the event that you are ever invited to progress beyond the 33rd Degree. I would like to be the one tasked with introducing you to Lucifer. I expect you will likely come back and say how there is no further progression beyond 33rd. Well, if you're lucky, there will be a nice surprise in store for you, somewhere down the line. I sincerely hope that make it that far.

ATS: That your repeating debunked conspiracy theory shows your just here to hoax.

HH: That word "debunked" always brings me a hearty laugh. Some people seem to think that throwing the word "debunked" around means that it really has been. The vast majority of "debunking" has more holes in it that the "conspiracy theories" it's meant to be silencing. Just enough of a "shell" to help those who really don't want the Truth to be True, to carry on believing that it's not, so they can replace their heads back into the sand for a while longer.

Anyway, I must press on with questions from those with open minds, I leave you with my regards, keep up your good work.

. . .

ATS: Over the course of my life I have occasionally resorted to prayer, some formal & some not with truly astounding & nearly instant physical results. I've taken these results to heart as personal evidence that some higher force or forces can respond in a meaningful manner to at least me & perhaps to anyone; Still, I don't rule out the possibility of coincidence. From your vantage point, would you please be gracious enough to shed light on this phenomena

HH: There is no such thing as coincidence. Nothing happens by chance.

Life is in a constant process of communication with us. Only mostly, people are too busy to notice.

Our Infinite Creator longs to be close to us. In truth, he is closer than most would believe, they just don't notice him. As they pass him by on the street every day, when he gives them their change at the shop, when you tuck her into bed and give her a kiss goodnight, when you squash him as he's running up your bathroom wall toward his web. When there's no-one else in the room but 'you'.

The main reason people don't have their "prayers" answered, is because they do not really believe that they will. Don't have "faith" in our Infinite Creator, have Trust in him. **The most Powerful form of "prayer", is Thanksgiving. "For even before you ask, I have already given it unto you".** Thanksgiving, is knowing that our Infinite Creator has provided for you as he promised, and being thankful for that, even before you see the results. The more we trust in our Creator, the more results we get.

Life gives us what we expect we'll receive. (Because all thought is Creative). If we get up, and expect to have a bad day, more often than not, that's exactly what we'll get.

But remember, that it works both ways.

ATS: And this one would be the hoaxer's sock puppet (new name, all posts in this thread, acting as the coach for the OP), created to give him/her the aura of credibility.

HH: Oh dear. You really are desperately clutching at straws. Any Admin can have the power to see if I'm using multiple accounts. I would be more than happy for an Admin to say if I am. Because I am not. Two accounts will show for me. "Hidden-Hand", my first one that I never got the confirmation email for, and this one, "Hidden_Hand", the one I did get the confirmation for.

My Infinite Creator gives me the only "credibility" that I need, or that I want, for that matter.

ATS: Hidden_Hand, I've enjoyed reading your posts if for nothing then the unusual (for ATS "whistleblowers" anyway) fact that it isn't bullet holed with bad writing, grammer and typos. May I respectfully recomend that you choose another venue next time? (I like ProjectCamelot myself). In anycase I'm still reading with an open mind but sceptical mind.

HH: Thank you. We are aware of Project Camelot. They are doing some remarkable work. Though I was not aware they also have a forum, if that's what you are suggesting? Not really my area usually, dealing with the internet. In fact I rarely have time to even venture onto it. I have quite enjoyed this time of relating to others over "cyber-space".

Well, if you're game for an "assignment", or maybe someone else if you haven't the time, I would be happy for someone to collate this topic (minus the "interruptions") so that the message appears with just the actual flow of questions and answers, and post it there in one piece, if you so desire. As I mentioned before, I chose ATS as I was reliably informed that it is one of the forums with a higher rate of intelligence and reasoning amongst it's members. On the whole, from my experience here, I would tend to agree.

Though if you think it would be of value to Camelot, by all means you are most welcome to spread this message. The more people it can reach, the better.

ATS: I have very few dreams now a days, but I had one last night, and it urged me to pose a question to you. I find it amazing that out of all the topics the universe has to offer, it offers me this

HH: Nothing by chance sir, nothing by chance.

Dreams are a key method our Souls use to speak with us. The conscious mind is too busy and distracted most of the time, to hear what Spirit has to say. So It tends to use the subconscious instead.

ATS: Hidden_Hand, I have, for my whole life searched near and far for answers to questions.

When I read your words I am compelled from within to explore their complete meanings and truthfulness. I am forced to examine them to the fullest. And I am charged with comparing them to the truth within me.

HH: That is precisely that way it should be. Again, I would encourage you NOT to just blindly accept what I say as "the truth". It never was my intention that anyone should make such an error in judgment. That is not to say that my words are not True, but that one must weigh them up, meditate upon them, and decide for yourself in the light of your intuition and inner feelings, whether or not these words "feel" True for you.

ATS: Hidden Hand, my question I pose to you, with the greatest respect and humility, Who will you stand before when we are all called home?

HH: We shall stand as all shall, before our One Infinite Creator.

We already know that which awaits us, in our coming 4th Density Negative Polarity world. **We shall have to experience the Negativity of our own creation, and know what it feels like. We shall have to work off the Karmic effect of our actions**. But at the same time, knowing that this is a beautiful and intricate game that we are all co-creating here together, we also know that we shall be rewarded with a hearty "thank you" and "job well done", for the Sacrifice we have made, in bringing this Negative Polarity into your Game for you, that you may use it wisely, to see that which you are not.

Thank you for your questions, we wish you all the very best, and ask our Infinite Creator to bless your path.

ATS: As you will be leaving us this Friday I would be interested in finding verification for other possible sources of information for this knowledge. You have mentioned the "RA" chanelings, but I also see similarities in three other sources which have been discussed in this and other forums on the internet. I would appreciate your evaluation of the information coming from these sources in the light of your messages. They are ACIM (A course in Miracles, alledgedled channeled by the Christos), The Edgar Cayce Material (In which the RA entity may have played a part), and the "Terra Papers". Can those of us seeking to continue our understanding of these matters find anything of use from these sources?

HH: ACIM has some core truths within it, mainly along the lines of the Law of Radiation and Attraction, but it is also littered with inaccuracies.

I am not aware of "the Terra Papers".

Edgar Cayce's work is significant. There are many distortions within it, but for ones who are of a discerning mind, there is much strong meat to be ingested from it's reading. Keep an open mind, but weigh it all up (as you should any philosophy that you allow to enter into the sacred space of your mind) and take the Truths that resonate with you.

ATS: Also you mentioned 2 prior contacts (1999 and 2003) can you shed some more light and specifics on those sources as I assume they are not to be considered privileged to those who ask?

HH: Unfortunately that is beyond my remit. The 2003 material was removed by the Admins of the site it was shared at as they felt it was "causing too much controversy", and the 1999 material was not released for the same reasons as that which I am sharing here. There was much Truth within it, but our goals have changed in many ways since that time, and it would be misleading for me to point you in it's direction now, in fact I have been specifically instructed by my own upline not to do so. I am sorry.

ATS: Thank you for your assistance,

Namasté

HH: You are welcome. That is a wonderful word to have ended your communication with.

If one would genuinely live by it's essence, "to recognize and honour the divine spark within each of us" we would be in for a massively Positive Harvest.

Namasté to you too. We ask that our One Infinite Creator blesses you, and guides your path.

ATS: I wonder if Hidden_Hand has read something called The Law of One. I've only picked through it (having just stumbled on it after reading these posts)...but it reads remarkably similar to H_H's responses here.

www.lawofone.info ...

So is this the hoax source, or is that book instead the "truth?" Maybe H_H could respond...?

HH: I have already made reference to this (The Ra material) earlier in the topic.

As I stated then, yes, it is the most accurate public information available in this world currently, and I strongly recommend it's reading, to anyone with an enquiring mind.

I read some, but not all of the books when they first came out, some 25 years or so ago, and it is very similar to the knowledge my Family has, and have passed down for many many generations.

It is approximately 85-90% accurate. The inaccuracies occurred when the channel was weak, and were not intentional. **We know Ra (the entity) very well, and are happy that they are even now still working here on this planet "behind the scenes" to prepare for the Great Harvest.**

I think I'm up to date with your questions now, if I have missed any (that are not unimportant ones, such as what car I drive for example), then please let me know.

We have two sessions left together, and then I must take my leave. Will look forward to seeing you tomorrow.

Fourth Session:

HH: Ok, as I stated, unfortunately my remaining time is shorter than planned. This was unforeseen and unavoidable. I will not have sufficient time to answer all of your questions, so I will for the most part, focus my remaining time with you, upon responding to those questions that I feel to be from the heart, ones asked by those who are genuinely looking to take something away with them of import from our discourse here together. My second focus will be upon answering other intelligent or insightful questions that can be used to further develop our discourse. I desire to impart as much as I am able with you, in the short time we have left. I will also, as far as possible, answer other questions that I feel are important in the grand scheme of things, meaning that even if the question seems to be from someone more intent on finding things to "debunk", if that question ultimately still serves a greater purpose, I will do my best to reply.

Please bear in mind, that in light of the above, many of my answers will need to exercise more brevity that I would ideally like, though this is necessary, to respond to as many of you as I can..

Without further delay, I shall continue with our discourse:

ATS: Do you know me? Do you know who i'm? What part do i play in all this? When will i awake? Will i awake? Should i awake? I feel it in me, but i'm afraid to let it out? Help me!

HH: Do I "know" you, as the individuated human expression typing to me over cyberspace? No, I do not.

What part do you play in all this?

What part do you want to play? The choice, as always, is entirely yours. Whether you are consciously aware of it or not, you are co-creating the storyline on this planet. My advice, would be to do so consciously.

When will you awake?

When do you want to awake? Do you want to awake at all? If your answer to this question is "yes", then use the Catalyst and tools we have provided for you. I have made many subtle, not so subtle, and even overtly blatant statements within this topic, as to how you may choose to do this.

"I feel it in me, but i'm afraid to let it out? Help me!"

Why are you afraid? Do not reply to that question, but rather, ask it to yourself, during your quiet time, where you work upon yourself. **You do work upon yourself, don't you? If not, now would be a good time to start. Sit in silence. Switch off all non essential electrical appliances. Eg; leaving the refrigerator on, would probably be a good idea. (The electromagnetic field they create disturbs your brainwave patterns, and makes it difficult for your mind to achieve the deeper alpha and theta states conducive with relaxing deeply and hearing your inner voice).**

Ask your Infinite Creator to help you. Thank her, because you know that he will.

Be honest with yourself. Why are you afraid? Remember that this is a Game that you are playing, and that it is not Reality. **When you find, and come to know your Creator living within you, you will know that there is nothing to fear.**

Be the strong and courageous Soul that deep down, you know yourself to be. Do not hide your Inner Light. Trust yourself, and shine your light into the darkness.

We ask our One Infinite Creator to guide you, and illuminate your path.

ATS: Are the PTB [**Powers That Be,** *Wes Penre's comment*] focusing on creating a negative point in the universe to upset the balance of our universe?

HH: No.

ATS: **Was the 911 ritual the creation of a star gate?**

HH: **No, it was a Ritual Human Sacrifice. That, and the obvious catalyst for the so called "War on Terror".**

ATS: So could the predictions of federation of light's "Goodchild" could have been true in a sense instead of a UFO or our understanding of a UFO could be light bearers influencing mankind ascend / descend to a higher/lower vibration status?

HH: She has a good heart. She just tuned into the "wrong channel" and listened to the wrong programme. I mentioned before, that if one does not exercise the appropriate protection, and discernment, what was initially a positive channel can very easily become unknowingly corrupted by a negative one. When they start giving you dates and times, you know that something is amiss. **Giving dates and times that are not going to come to pass, succeeds in putting out the Light of the 'channeller's message, by destroying the credibility of the messenger.**

ATS: Is the creation of fear, terror, horror and suffering by your kind to create loosh emotions for feeding at the time of harvest?

HH: No.

ATS: Are the bloodlines that have been infused with the ancient wisdoms trying to become god's themselves?

HH: There is no need to try. Humanity needs to grow beyond the stagnating concept of "gods". The idea of "god" takes the Power out of your own hands, and places it upon some shadowy unknown figure, somewhere "out there". In other words, outside of yourself. Instead of "god", see "Creator".

So, there is no need to "try".

We already are Creators. And so are you. The only question is, will you Create Consciously, or sub-consciously?

ATS: What is 11.11?

HH: Think of it as an alarm clock. What are alarm clocks for?

ATS: Please explain how new born babies are infused with spirits after birth.

HH: They are not. A Soul enters into It's physical container usually long before the birthing process, sometimes later, but still before the actual birth..

ATS: Does a website like this serve the purpose of negative generating?

HH: That depends upon how you use it. It has the potential to be either negative or positive.

It is up to you how you use the potential.

ATS: What is wrong with having an ego and why do the new age religions try to suppress the ego? Without an ego is seems as though one can't ponder his own existence. Or in fact learn from the wealth of knowledge that we are searching for in making mistakes and correcting those mistakes.

HH: There is nothing "wrong" with having an ego.

Your ego is an excellent and invaluable tool. Yet, as with any tool, if you do not have it under control, it carries the potential to become dangerous, and do you and others much harm.

ATS: H.H., strangely, my concern is that I will be recycled back onto the wheel of life and be reborn with a new brain and lose everything I have so arduously learned in this life time.

HH: **Your Soul remembers everything you've ever experienced**. The only reason you don't remember it all now, is due to what we term the "veil of forgetfulness". **If you came into each new incarnation with access to your Soul memory, there's no point in your coming into space/time**. It would be like playing a computer game with all the cheats. You wouldn't learn anything, and it takes the fun out of playing the game. Remember that this current physical body you carry around with you, is not who you are. It's just the vessel for your essence. Who you are, is Real, and cannot be destroyed. You will retain all your memories of this life experience once you pass onto the realm of time/space, or that which some call "Heaven". **space/time is illusion, time/space is Real**. That Infinite Being living within and around your "body", namely your Soul, is who you really are. The part of you that thinks, and feels, and loves. It will always be a part of you.

ATS: My dream is to be a master such as yourself.

HH: I am not a Master. I am a growing and evolving Soul, just as you are. We're just at different stages of our development. You will get to where you desire to be. It takes time and patience. Be sure to make time to enjoy the journey.

ATS: I endeavor each day to master myself and change. To develop a mind that has mastery over my body. I feel I have come so far in this life time and yet not far enough.

HH: You are on the right path, in that you are consciously choosing to work upon yourself. Many there are in this world, who are not even aware of such a concept. Remember though, that it is not only the mind you must develop, but also your Soul. Work with your feelings as well as your thoughts. **Cultivate Compassion (as that is the main thing you will begin working with in 4th Density). See yourself within all "others", and treat "others" as you would like to be treated yourself.** Then remember this one crucial thing:

There are no "others".

ATS: My dream is to one day personally meet great masters like yourself and learn what you know.

HH: Then here is what you must do:

Go and find yourself a mirror. Gaze deeply into it, and then say this magic word:

'Hello".

And you will indeed meet with us, back stage, once the game is over. When you see us "out of costume" you will recognize us as your age old friends.

ATS: Thank you for coming here and sharing your vast knowledge of the universe. I have much to ponder.

HH: You are welcome. Thank you for your questions. I feel the desire within you to progress. You have it Within yourSelf, to be all that you wish to become, and much more that you cannot yet even imagine.

We look forward to sitting down for a good old reminisce with you on the other side. In the meantime, keep Trusting in, and working upon yourself, and live each moment in Thanksgiving, to our One Infinite Creator.

May our Infinite Creator bless and guide your path.

ATS: Honored sir (or madam)

I wish to be the one to bring a new planetary energy system to the world. As it is assumed that the "families" have great knowledge, I humbly request access to this small bit of needed information.

A U2U message to set up a more secure route of communication would be splendid, I presume.

I am aware I can never be a "member", but "acolyte" would suffice.

I am also aware a trade off would be in the offing, and discussions of such would be held with respect, though not with guaranteed acceptance.

I await your reply.

HH: I am sorry, that this is not possible. One is Born into the Family, and raised in a very specific and rigorous way, which engenders unwavering Loyalty. No matter how keen and sincere one may be to "join" us, we can only place our trust in those raised in our ways. **I would not wish the conditioning process we go through on anyone, it can be grueling at times, and it is too late to begin the process once childhood has passed.**

As for further communication, unfortunately this is also not possible or allowable for me.

I have given as much information as is permissible for me, during this discourse. There are many informational "gems" within these pages, for those who truly seek to develop themselves. Some are obvious, others are more subtle and multi-layered. Take them "within", and ask your Infinite Creator to bring you insight.

We wish you well upon your journey, and look forward to seeing you at the "aftershow" party.

ATS: I'm still not clear on what this harvest is. A "harvest" means to reap what has been sown - by you!

HH: Not by us. We did not sow, our Infinite Creator did. We do not reap, our Infinite Creator does.

We help to prepare the Harvest, by separating the wheat from the chaff, for want of a more eloquent metaphor.

ATS: Will it be an instantaneous change, of which there will no longer exist the physical realm as we currently know it to be and are experiencing as an "illusion"?

HH: I have already covered this elsewhere in the topic. I would encourage you to read through again, and find the information I have already presented on how the Harvest will occur, and what the different variations of experience will be.

ATS: Thank you for answering my previous questions. I have some more, if that's ok?

1. How can karma be overcome, if at all? Is there an end to the karmic cycle?
2. Is time really as we perceive it, or is it another 3D illusion?
3. Are your family members born with the knowledge of what they are and where they're from? If not, and it's all taught and passed down, have you ever doubted or questioned any of it?

Thanks.

HH: You are welcome.

1). No, **Karma cannot be 'overcome', it must be 'worked off'**. In other words, if you've hurt someone, be it physically, emotionally, or however else, you will have to, at some future point, experience what that felt like for them. **The Law of Karmic Effect is not a 'punishment', it is a tool of learning**, which is set in place to promote personal growth and development. If you have to feel the consequences of your actions, there is a higher likelihood of your choosing a different course, the next time around. It is also important to hold in mind that it works both ways. Seek therefore to ensure that the effect of your presence upon those 'others' whom you encounter upon your journey, are positive and beneficial.

1b). **A Karmic Cycle is brought to completion once you have learned the lessons intended for you from it. If you keep repeating the same mistakes, you'll keep cycling until such a time as you get the message, and break the cycle. But yes, ultimately, all of us will learn that which we need to learn, and all of us will find our way Home. For some, it just takes longer than others.**

2). **Linear time is** more accurately described as **an intentional fabrication. The true nature of time, is cyclical**. Though, remember also, that **even cyclical time, is part of Creation, and Creation, beautiful as it may be, is also an Illusion, or more accurately, a Thought-Form of our Infinite**

Creator. Creation is not Real, but the Creator and Co-Creators of it, are.

2). This is an excellent question. I will devote some time to it:

Firstly, there is a distinction to be made. **When I speak of Family in this particular reply, I am referring to the Power lines, ie; those that do not originate from this planet.** The bloodlines that you know of, whilst they are a part of our extended Family, are not born with the same extent of (Spiritual/Esoteric) Power that we are, and in this response, I am referring to our True and Pure Family. We are not born with the same veil of forgetfulness as you are. The veil is still in place, but would be most accurately described as being somewhat "thinner". We see the "invisible" connections of life which are hidden from you, because **we retain access to more than just the 3rd Density perspective**. Not dissimilar to the manner in which some people can see what you call auras. This is because **you are working your way up, whereas we have chosen to step down, in order to help you**. We could not do this as successfully if we had to forget all that we have learned. In other words, to you, everything "appears" as being "separate". We see that this is not the case. **We do not have 'direct' Soul Memory, as in the manner that you remember what you did yesterday, but we may access any portion of our Soul memory we so chose when we focus upon it, often in a meditative state.** Personally, my experiences are different again, in other ways, due to my specialty in the Spiritual disciplines. But I will go into that in more detail later, in response to another question.

Yes, information is indeed passed down, though unlike for yourselves, any one of us may, with some effort, check the validity of that information from our Personal and Group Soul Memory. basically, where you see yourselves as "separate" human beings, we see and Know, that we are One.

ATS: Then I am glad I picked up on that particular point. I found it to be a real ray of light. Though, I'm unsure what to do with it. This information feels as though it should comfort me, and yet it's difficult to feel comfortable knowing that 'evil', in part, makes us who we are. But thank you nonetheless.

HH: **"Evil" is Not who you are. It is part of the complex series of illusions, that you use in 3rd Density, to show you who you are not.** The further up through the Densities you work, the less Polarity plays an important part in the game. **The Sixth Density, the Density of Unity, is the last level that Polarity is a factor, but even then, it factors in a very different way. Instead of balancing Positive / Negative, you will be balancing Love / Light, Compassion / Wisdom.**

ATS: True, and I'm glad you pointed that out to me. I think what I really meant when I said you are "alleviated" is that your very essence is not 'evil' or corrupt. And this alleviates you from my perspective because I'd forged an idea of the ruling elite as being comprised of terminally corrupted souls.

HH: No Soul is terminally corrupted. Every Soul is a beautiful individuated portion of our One Infinite Creator. Souls play characters in the Game of Incarnation. Souls can play some really mean and nasty characters, but underneath the disguise, they will always be beautiful. Remember this, everytime one of these beautiful Souls 'mistreats' you as a part of their storyline. They're just playing their part, like any good actor does whilst on stage. Be thankful to them for their Sacrifice, and learn the lessons they are bringing to you.

ATS: You say we all mingle between incarnations but I suspect the nature of our perception and interaction in that realm is not comparable to our Earthly methods of interaction and therefore, as a united entity there'll be no independent 'laughter' . I have a few (what I feel are probably final) questions for you:

HH: Not so. **Think in terms of individuated Souls, who can see and understand that they are not separate, but interconnected. It is an illusion, that "space" is "empty". You will still interact as** an individual, yet at the same time, you will see how we are all One. It is difficult to explain in a way that makes 3rd Density sense. We just do not have the words or concepts to describe it.

We no longer need words where we are going.

ATS: 1) How do you know all this? And I really mean KNOW. Clearly you have been taught in great depth about the nature of existence. But how do you know this first hand? How is it more than faith for you? Have you been able to avoid 'forgetting' upon reincarnation?

HH: I have made reference to this, in my answer to the previous poster.

ATS: 2) You seem to be suggesting that your methods of physical enslavement are intended to force us into spiritual awakening. But if that is so, why are methods of spiritual suppression used against the general populace (chemicals, organised religion, sociological)? I understand why you obstruct our material lives but not why you obstruct our spiritual development.

HH: **Think of it as a "test".**

Have you ever noticed, how just when you 'think' you've found something that really "feels" like Truth for you, something will come along to make you doubt it? To make you doubt the truth, and in so doing, to also doubt yourself in believing it?

It happens all the time, in fact, almost every time you have some new revelation that gets you all excited. And it happens, quite by design. You cannot see this however, as it's happening beyond 3rd Density comprehension, in a realm where everything can be seen as adjoining and relating to everything else. Syncronicity. All a magical part of our Infinite Creator's ingenously Creative mind, and excellent sense of humour and irony.

Can you see how the "test" works?

Just when you find something that you've weighed up and dissected with your discernment, and decided to integrate it into your concept of "Truth", along comes the challenge to your newfound beliefs. Usually in the form of an event, or something that 'others' may say to disuede you.

Your Spiritual development, like all other aspects of your progression, is something that you have to work for. How do you know if your newly discovered 'truth' is really True, if you're never tested on it.

The test, is this:

In the face of a challenge, who do you trust?

Do you trust what the "outside world" is showing you?

Or, do you hold fast to that which "feels" like Truth, deep within you?

That is something you can only answer for yourself.

I am sorry I do not have the time left to respond to all of your questions, so I selected the ones I felt to be the most important.

I have enjoyed our communication Cythraul, and am happy to have made your aquaintance.

Well, I must press on with more questions. I ask that our Infinite Creator bless and guide you on your path, and give you the Courage of your convictions.

Be well friend, I look forward to meeting up with you when we've completed the game.

ATS: I have one more question for you if i may.

What question has not been asked as of yet that is most important for us to know if any? And if there is any would you consider it asked now? Not sure if this one does any good but it stuck in my mind last night.

HH: An excellent, and incisive question to ask.

I think what I shall do, is to save this question, for the very end of our discourse.

It will be an effective way to bring our time together to a close.

ATS: Hidden_Hand, I know you're trying to focus on spiritual questions and questions about the density shift. But if you could detract for a moment to answer my questions about shape shifting I'd appreciate it.

HH: I will, but must be very brief, I am sorry.

Shapeshifting is not a "natural" phenomenon. "Shapeshifting" creatures / races do not exist, at least certainly not in any realm, Galaxy or Density we have ever experienced.

However, there are certain Rituals that when engaged in, enables this to take place.

It has to do with the fact that the body, as is true of all physical things, is not really solid. Sure, it looks and feels as if it is, but in actuality, all matter is composed of atomic and sub-atomic particles of Light, within molecules and compounds. As I say, I'm being brief through necessity, and don't have time to go into the science.

There are certain Rituals which when undertaken, allow for a range of 'manipulations' of the so-called 'solid' bodily mass to take place. I have seen some grotesque images in my time, which I really prefer not to dwell upon.

I trust that even if in some small way, this will have answered your query.

And this next question, I will have to finish on for tonight. I have somewhere I must be.

ATS: H_H, I wish to thank you for your enlightening words. It has been an utmost pleasure of mine to read what you have spoken.

I do however have a couple of questions..

As I look into myself, I see (feel) as though I am an old soul who has learned many things and possibilities, how are we to know how far along we have come in regards to obtaining a higher spiritual being during the coming Harvest?

HH: You are most welcome. Appreciation is always appreciated.

I am unsure whether your question refers to now, or once the Great Harvest is accomplished, I've already touched on what happens after in a few replies. so I'll go with the former.

As for now, there is a simple method to check upon your progress.

Despite what "appears" to being going on in "the world at large", how loving and harmonious are your personal relationships?

Remember that the world, is your mirror. Casting back at you the reflection, of that which you have projected into it. How many arguments do you find yourself engaging in? Is there bitterness and acrimony within the ranks? Do you look at others, and think about how you would like to change them? Or, do you love them, and accept them as they are?

Loving and accepting someone, for who they are, is known as Unconditional Love. That is something you will spend much time working upon, when Graduating into 4th Density Positive. It's a good idea to get a headstart. Now, loving and accepting someone as they are, does not mean accepting abusive behavior. But, it does mean loving and accepting the person (Soul), not the Soul's behavior. The behavior is not "who they are", the Soul within, is who they are.

The quality of your relationships, is an excellent mirror, from which to gauge the quality of your output. Or, in other words, that which you are Creating.

Do you look at a person, and concentrate to a greater or lesser extent, upon the things that you dislike about them and wish would change, or the qualities that you like and admire in them?

Remember that we have said, that all thought, word, and deed, is Creative.

You get back Exactly what you send out.

So, when you send out the thought "Why is she so hard to live with? Why is he always behaving like this?

Ask yourself, what exactly are you doing?

Now focus here, as this is so obvious, you could miss it. And in fact, most do.

Take away the "question" from your sentence, and essentially, you are saying:

"She is so hard to live with". "He is always behaving like this".

Do you see what you are doing?

Remember, All thought is creative..

You have just created the very behaviour in that person, that you wish to change. Simply because you do not understand the Law of Radiation and Attraction.

Now, try an experiment:

Take someone in your life, that you love, but sometimes have trouble getting along with.

Think, about the thoughts you have projected about that person. The Negative thoughts. Ask yourself, does the behavior that you do not like in that person, in any way correspond to the thoughts you have been having about them? If you're honest with yourself, it's a strong bet that it does.

Sure, they must have behaved that way in the first place, to make you notice that you didn't like it, but, we all have off days sometimes. The more you focus on that behavior, the more you are going to see of it. It's just Life, doing what it does, and conforming to your expectations about the way it will be for you.

Now, having recognized this, what will you do about it?

Simply notice your Negative thoughts as they arise, literally, "catch yourself" as you are having them. And then, simply change your perspective. Focus instead, about the things you like about this person. How you love their smile, the sound of their happy laughter; the way they do such and such nice thing, how helpful and loving they can be. Keep putting those positive thoughts out. Persevere, as you may have a bit of negative work to undo first, but just keep catching yourself, and focusing on the positive..

Then prepare yourself for an "almost magical" transformation of your circumstances.

Always monitor your thoughts, and pay attention to their Quality; because what you think about, is directly related to what you will see around you, and what Life will show you. It is the difference between conscious, and subconscious Creation.

ATS: And what of our Loved Ones, or more appropriately, my soul mate who I Love dearly. Will I be able to take this new Journey of the Harvest alongside my Loved ones?

HH: That will depend upon whether or not you both Graduate, or have to repeat the cycle. Though rest assured, even if for one lifetime you were to be apart, you will always be together in time/space (between incarnations) and you will be able to plan many future 'lives' (incarnations) together.

ATS: And one more thing as I know there are others who are longing for questions answered..

Why do we Dream in Metaphors which make no sense?

HH: I do not have time left tonight to respond sufficiently, but the short version is that the Universal Mind speaks in Archetypal Imagery. In a similar way that the writing in some of our Oriental languages uses a system whereby a collection of words or meanings are contained within what is essentially a 'symbol', so the Universal Mind uses Archetypes to communicate in Dreamtime. Just like understanding any new dialect, you just need to learn the language.

ATS: Thank you so very much H_H, I strongly wish I may meet you someday and have a good talk.

HH: You are very welcome, and it will happen as you wish.

Not now, in this lifetime, but soon, when we have finished playing this game together. No rush though friend, we've got all the time/space in the world. All the time/space in Creation actually.

I must go now for tonight. I shall do my best to reply to as many of you as I possibly can do tomorrow, before I must take my leave.

Goodnight to you all. I ask that our Infinite Creator bless and watch over you.

Fifth Session:

HH: This will be our last session together.

I will do my very best to pack in as much as we can.

I am sorry for those who must have missed my earlier post from yesterday which clearly stated that I already have more questions than I have time to answer, and that you have spent the time in writing our new ones. My time is so limited, I am unable to respond to you. I have a long journey I must make shortly, and cannot be late for it.

ATS: I have always been very confused and not clear on the subject of "god", having been tossed around from religion to religion from my parents it is hard to discern which "god" to believe or have faith in. Should I keep on having faith in the fact that the world around me is "god" and that there is not one particular being that deserves this faith?

HH: **Religion is either actually created, or at very least, heavily influenced by us**. There is no such things as "god". **"God" is a human concept, which is a misunderstanding of the original concept of "Creator"**. This is further confused, as there are **many macrocosmic level Creators, or Logos, as has been explained previously**. "God" implies some separate entity which is 'outside' of you, which you must supplicate to and worship. **Our One Infinite Creator, and almost all of our Logos and sub-Logos', do not want your worship. They want you to understand Creation, and your place within it, as a Co-Creator.** Ultimately, **there is a "Supreme Being", in the form of the One Infinite Creator, but we are all a part of It, rather than it's subjects.** None of the names given for this "Supreme Being" by your religions are the true name, but they are indeed correct, in that there is One Supreme Being, namely the Infinite Creator. They just have different concepts about It, which spring from the texts their religion is based upon.

Do not 'worship' your Infinite Creator, but rather live in a state of Thanksgiving and Service to It, for bringing you into Being, and for this amazing Game It has Created, in which we may forget who we really are, in order to remember, and know ourself one again, as the Creator.

ATS: So basically the form that we have is actually just a body with bones and skin and so on and so forth, what matters is our soul or being that is inside us that makes us question and deal with our surroundings and life, so when we "die" the pain and suffering is just part of our human shell, and has nothing to do with our soul or being which will carry on into the next life or density?

HH: Indeed. 'pain' and 'suffering' are just aspects of the Game. They feel extremely real whilst we are playing the Game, and indeed they have to, in order to make you believe that the Game is real. No-one really "dies". But rather, the 'matter' of human form is shed, much like the chrysalis of a caterpillar, when the butterfly emerges. Look upon physical incarnation as the chrysalis in which you may transform.

ATS: I feel as though I am like Shelby, but have lost my way, or I am just so confused and not in-tune with my inner-self that I can not figure out what is my purpose in this game. Is there anything you can shed upon this?

HH: **Your purpose in the Game, is to work upon yourself**. To grow, develop, and transform yourself into a more positive and loving being. **You had certain goals that you planned to achieve before incarnating here**, which is a main reason for the veil of forgetfulness being in place, because if you already knew what your goals were, the Game would be too easy.

Look at the things in your life that you most love to do. Ask yourself what makes you most happy. Experience these things as often as possible, as they will be related to some of the things you chose to put into your Soul contract to do here.

Also, look at the negative things, that often seem to recur during your lifetime. It will be highly likely that these are also things that you chose to come here to work upon. Let us say for example, that you chose to come here to work upon patience during this incarnation. You will likely find that you have a tendency towards impatience, and that life will often bring many experiences to you, in order to 'test' your patience. The idea being, that rather than losing your temper, you work upon your impatience, and resolve to become a more temperate and patient Soul.

This same analogy may be applied to all manner of circumstances in which life will test you. Look for and begin to identify any recurring issues you have, that you perhaps struggle to deal with, and seem to present themselves to you, time and time again. Perhaps anger, being abusive, selfishness, hatred, cynicism, and the list goes on. Whenever you find recurring circumstances, it is because you are being presented with opportunity after opportunity, to work upon these issues, until you get it right, and choose a way of behavior that is more Positive. Once you've successfully identified these issues within your life, worked upon them, and used them as the tools of transformation that they are, to improve the quality of your character, you will notice that these things seem to almost cease to appear in your life. You will still be presented with them at varying intervals, to check that you have not forgotten that which you have learned, but they will be fewer and far between.

I hope this may give you some clues as to how to identify the things you came here to do, and how to go about working upon yourself.

ATS: My life has been a troubled one for awhile now, having been so soaked and brainwashed into the human life form and way of life, but lately I feel as though I am starting to wake up and see things more clearly. Am I doomed because of the path I have taken for most of my life, or can I still save my "soul"?

HH: **You are not 'doomed', and your Soul does not require 'salvation'. No-one's Soul does.** There is nothing to 'save' it from. It is good to hear that you are awakening, and that is another reason why I am here at this time, speaking with you. Our Infinite Creator has many messengers, and he uses us all in our own unique ways, to help with the Awakening, and prepare as many as possible, for the coming Great Harvest.

But as I say, you are not 'doomed', and there is nothing to save yourself from, except perhaps, from ignorance. And I do not mean that in an insulting way, but rather, ignorance as in a 'lack of understanding'. **At the very worst, you will have to repeat as many 3rd Density Cycles as is necessary, in order for you to learn the things you need to learn, in order to progress and Graduate to 4th Density Positive. But one thing is for sure, you will get there in the end.** All will find their way Home, to our Infinite Creator. Rest also assured, that you will not find yourself 'lost' in your cycling. **At the end of each physical incarnation, as I've previously stated, you return to** time/space, or that which has been described as "Heaven", where you shall once again know yourself as you truly are, a unique and beautiful Soul, and a part of our Creator. You only forget who you are during incarnation.** The object of the Game, is to wake up within the 'dream', and in effect, become a 'Lucid Gamer'. To remember who you really are during the Game, and to then begin working upon the things you came here for. Re-reading this topic, with discernment, will provide you with plenty of clues on how you may choose to go about this.

ATS: Thank you for your time here with us, and I wish you the best, it has been a pleasure speaking with you and listening to your knowledge.

HH: We wish the same for you Brother, and ask that our Infinite Creator bless you and guide your path. See you when we get Home.

ATS: So, is the harvest an "all or nothing" event or will it be a mixed harvest—a few moving to fourth density, a few moving towards fourth density in service to self, the great majority repeating third density? And if only 94% go to fourth density negative, then you have to repeat 3rd density and try again for a 95% negative harvest? If so, then I would hate to imagine how much more negative your people would make the earth at that point.

I'm still confused about your part in this. In order for you to move on the 4th level, it must be a 95% negative harvest. In other words, to reward your people with 4th density, 95% of the human souls have to be (in the self-contemplation process) as far away from the "Infinite Source" as humanly possible. That just doesn't "feel" right to me.

HH: It does not 'feel' right to you, as it is not right. You have not entirely grasped the concept. I shall attempt to clarify.

The Harvest is Mixed. Those who are 51% or over on the Positive path will Graduate to 4th Density Positive. There you will work upon Love and Compassion, and it will be a very beautiful world to reside within for you. There will be very little negativity. Just a small enough amount that you can still use it to exercise your Free Will in choosing who you are not, but it will be so much more obvious than it is here, that the negativity is a tool to be used. You will see the interconnectedness of all things, and you will know that you are not 'separate' from one another, or from life Itself. You will not use words much, unless you choose to. **Telepathy becomes the normal method of communication. Everything is open, and you cannot hide your thoughts from 'others'.**

From that incarnation onwards, you will not have to experience 3rd Density incarnation again, unless you later choose to do so from Higher Densities, as we have done, in order to perfect the art of Service, or unless you somehow, in a 4th Density world of abundant love and beauty, inextricably manage to be 95% Negative at a time of future Harvest, and slide back down the snake, instead of ascending up the ladder, to use another 'Game' metaphor.

Back to 'this' current Great Harvest, **we do not require a 95% Negative Harvest, as you have deducted. Instead, what we require, is for US to personally attain a 95% Negative Polarity for ourselves, not for you. WE must be 95% Negative (at least), in order to Graduate to 4th Density Negative, and earn the opportunity to clear our Karmic Record, of all the Negativity we have Created on this planet, before returning to our rightful place as 6th Density Guardians of our Galaxy, and teachers of Wisdom to those in lower Densities that ask for our assistance.** If we do not make it, we will remain trapped in the 3rd Density Cycle with all those between 94% Negative and 50% Positive (what I termed 'luke-warm's'), and have to continue to provide Negative Polarity for you. Harsh as it is, our only way out, is to be as Negative as possible, to Graduate. We cannot choose to be

Positive, because that is not what we came here to do for you. **That's why I often have referred to all the horrible things we've done here, as our Sacrifice.**

ATS: You said that **the "lukewarm people" at the time of harvest** would not notice anything has happened, but they'd be on a different planet. Do you mean that they'd wake up with no memory of what has occurred but still be in the same physical body, or they'd wake up in a new physical body with no memory of any past life?

HH: **There will be a short experience of 'zero-point time', where you feel utterly "at One" with your Infinite Creator. It will be a feeling of blissful, ecstatic expansiveness and Unity, whilst your physical vehicles (bodies) are dissolved back into Light, and transported to your new environment. When that transition is complete, the 'zero-point time' will end, and you will 'appear' in your new 'game-zone' (planet). You will look the same, think the same, feel the same, in fact, it will be just like you all had some mystical experience, and life will carry on as 'normal' for you. Same houses, family situations, jobs, friends, lovers. Everything will seem the same as before, you will not remember the Great Harvest or earth changes that occurred as the planet Earth heals and regenerates herself. But you will recall your 'mystical experience' and that will give you hope and a new opportunity to choose a more positive future for yourselves.**

There will still be the same Negative Polarity to overcome, but if we are successful in our Negative Graduation, (which we shall be) others are standing by to take our places pulling the strings from "behind the scenes". We have more than done our job, in discharging our Service to you. And we are tired. It is time for us to clear our Karmic Record, and return to being the Being of Light which is our True essence.

ATS: You keep saying help is available to those searching for truth, all we have to do is ask. What is the best way to go about this? I have never had the ability to remember any of my dreams.

HH: Read back, I have given guidance on dream recall previously. it takes practice, and is a slow process, but you have to start somewhere, Be patient with yourself.

ATS: What specifically can I do to receive guidance on how to reach the state where it is easier to discern truth from untruth?

HH: **Work upon yourself. Go inside, in a state of meditative contemplation. Still your mind, that your Soul may have room in which to make It's 'still-small voice' heard. Ask your Infinite Creator to help you, and listen to your inner voice. Be patient, it takes time to develop this inner communication, after a lifetime of neglect. When you persevere and keep working on yourself, gradually it will come to you, and when it does, you must learn to TRUST in your Inner Guidance, NO MATTER WHAT OTHERS MAY SAY. That is the ultimate test. To Trust what you know deep inside as your Truth, even when the whole world tells you that you are "wrong". It is hard work, to Trust yourself when all those around you doubt you and call you crazy, but it is the job you came here to do.**

The only real and lasting Truth, is a 'self-realized' one. Messengers can come and go, and show you Truth until they're blue in the face, but it will not be Your Truth, until you have realized for yourself, deep within the Core of your Being, that it 'feels' True for you.

You should never accept something as true, just because someone tell you it is so. But when your inner voice guides you that a Truth is True, and you feel that old warm feeling of excitement welling up from somewhere deep within, that says "Yes! I knew it!" Hold on to that feeling, (feelings are the language of your Soul) and Guard it carefully, as you can be sure that your

newfound beliefs will be challenged in many ways. It is designed this way, to test you. Your Inner Truth must be able to withstand the test of time, and will be given a thorough examination. Hold fast to it, so long as it is what you Know to be True deep within. Allow nothing or no-one 'outside' of you to pull you from your path, no matter how fiercely they contend with you. They are just doing their job, even if they may well not even be 'aware' that this is what they are in fact doing. They are performing an important service to you, and you should be grateful to them for that.

We wish you well on your journey, and ask our Infinite Creator to protect and guide you upon your path.

"arc de triumphe":

I do not have the time to go into your many questions, so I will just select a few I can answer briefly, as I still have so many questions to get through.

ATS: Do the **Orion/occultist groups** specifically target civilizations before they become a social memory complex.

HH: Yes, but that does not make them immune to targeting others too, if they allow any chinks to appear in their armour. In short, **the Orion Empire are 4th Density Negative. They are "lost" in the sense that they have drifted so far from their true nature, that despite many attempts, we have been unable to reach them, and help them to develop.** They exist within their Group Soul Complex, mostly as a group of discarnate entities, within the Astral Planes of the planets they visit. They have no intention of 'returning Home', and instead seek to **feed off of Negative Energy**, to keep themselves going, as they are disconnected from their inherent natural Life-Force, by refusing to abide by the Infinite Creator's Incarnational Principles.

The time we spend between lives in time/space, is intended to restore our Soul Energy from within, in order to continue our upward progression. They are essentially 'imprisoned' within the 4th Density Negative cycle, as there is no Negative Harvest beyond the 4th Density. So they spend their time traveling the Galaxy, basically 'using the dark side of the Force' (Negativity) to achieve their means. They will eventually be brought back before the One Infinite Creator, and dissolved back into the Intelligent infinity (Source of All), though they are being given every chance for as long as possible, to learn the error of their ways, and return to seeking the Positive, and to begin their journey back Home. They main trouble is, they do not want to go Home. **They see themselves as being 'gods', and do not intend to submit to the authority of The One.**

ATS: Why all the sudden ramping up of control mechanisms.

HH: The Great Harvest is fast approaching. **Time to really bring on the Polar Extremes**.

ATS: **The Montauk Project....fact or fiction**.

HH: **The project is Fact. Though the publicly available information is in someways corrupted.**

ATS: Best ways to decipher between truth and fiction other than what we perceive to be truth specifically in concerning the New Age agenda and the dogmatic churches ideologies.

HH: Follow your Heart. Listen to, and Trust, your Inner voice.

ATS: Please explain the wanderer's roles and what value it is to be wanderer if you have no recollection of ones past lives. Also how does this play with the law of non-intervention (that's if they are here to help people).

HH: **The Wanderers, (or 'Travelers' as they are also known) are those from Higher Densities, who

have chosen to incarnate here at this time, in order to perfect Service to Others. They still have to 'remember who they are', and part of the concern, is that sometimes, even they do not manage to awaken in the Game, such is the power of the Illusion. They are here to awaken themselves, and then to help awaken others to prepare for the coming Great Harvest. Though even if they fail to awaken, they are not bound by the 3rd Density Cycle, as they've already mastered it. Once their incarnation is over, they are again free to return to their appropriate levels.

ATS: **Are there any non-corrupted parts of the bible and if what bible version would you suggest?**

HH: No. **As with all Sacred Texts, they have been distorted from the original information that was given with each translation.** Though again, as with all Sacred Texts, **there is still much truth hidden within them. Much of it being 'metaphorical'. If you can find pre King James versions, that is the closest you will get.** Good luck with that.

ATS: Was the Rothschild lineage the organizer of the Illuminati in which Weishhaupt later formed?

HH: No. **Weishhaupt was just a puppet on a string. The Rothschild lineage (not it's original name) were the pre-eminent line 'closing the net of control' over Humanity.** But even they, are a lesser line within The Family. As I have said, the names you know do not have the Real Power. They are part of the Family, but not an 'original' part.

ATS: My question is this: **what can I do to attract more like-minded individuals to come together to uplift my people's turning to the path of ascension. (I've decided that this is what I can do to express my personal act of 'service to others')**

HH: And a very wise and compassionate decision it is. We are proud of you.

The most important thing, is not to force things, and not to be so impassioned in your delivery of your message, that you put people off the content of the message itself. There is a balance that needs to be found, between your urgency to awaken others, and your compassion for the lack of understanding in their 'condition'. Always adhere to the Law of Free Will, and never force your message.

In getting your message out there, whilst being informative, always do your best not to feed the fear and paranoia, as this will act contrary to your intentions of raising the vibration to Positive. Deliver your message in a way that emphasizes the Hope, and the true beauty and reality of our inherent Oneness with our Infinite Creator. Be as a Light, shining in the Darkness. Do not burn others with your light, but rather, allow them to be drawn to your Light, and be of Service to those who come to you willingly. In other words, do not become 'evangelical' with your message, but rather, be the enigmatic and loving 'wise old sage', to whom others are drawn to because of the Quality of his vibration, rather than the volume of his rhetoric.

Most importantly, PRACTICE THAT WHICH YOU PREACH. Others must be able to see the effect of our Infinite Creator conducting his wonderful work through you.

We wish you well in your task, and are hopeful of a Positive Harvest for you. But above all things, keep working upon yourself, and keep choosing the Positive, and being of Service to others. Because you desire to, not because you feel that you must.

We ask our Infinite Creator to bless you and guide your path.

ATS: Earth Changes; While I understand that death is not the end of my existence, I like my body and would not like to get caught out in any earth changes if I can possibly help it.

1) If your family permits, please could you reveal **which places are more likely to be relatively safe during the next 3-4 years?** Would the South of China (Canton/Hong Kong) or Patagonia be good bets? Any other places?

HH: I am not permitted to say much here, as there must be those who remain in their locations, to help others who are not aware of what is coming. Many of you (whether you are aware or not) have chosen this lifetime for that reason.

But **if you are insistent upon escape, chose the Highest places you can find. Particularly in the Southern Hemisphere if you are able. The Peruvian Andes is a good place to be. There is much Spiritual Power being exercised there, and the Quero Elders are well aware of what is going down.**

ATS: 2) **Are John Lear/Jan Lamprecht correct in their assertion that the majority of planets of the Solar System are inhabited?**

HH: **Most definitely. Not all on a 3rd Density level that you can see though.**

ATS: **Is the Earth Hollow?**

HH: **Hold on, let me just check. Yes, definitely.**

ATS: If so, how does one gain access?

HH: I am not permitted to say.

ATS: Could you elaborate further on the mechanisms behind the fantastic positive results seen by people who embark on the service to others path? I invite you to really deeply explain the intricacies of the energy-play at work. While "You get out what you put in" is true, I'd like to see the whole concept dissected and fully explored.

HH: If you re-read some of my recent posts, I believe I have now done so.

ATS: I recently experienced healing of a minor health problem by sending love to all the sick people in the world. How does this work, not why, how.?!?!

HH: Because there is only ONE of you here.

Understand that, at a deep Core level of your Being, and you will understand how it works. As you do unto others, so you do to yourself.

ATS: **You claim your family was put here to be the negative influence of the world. Is there a family it is asserting a positive influence on us as well? Is it up to us (humanity) to be that positive force?**

HH: An interesting question. **There is such a family (or group more accurately), but you cannot see them, and neither are you aware of their existence. They help the planet from a secret "Inner" location, by the Quality of the Energy work they engage in and project outward to you, from the Source.**

Yes, it is up to you to Be the Changes you wish to see, in yourself, and in the World.

ATS: Your goal is a negative harvest, yet you clearly are touting the benefits of a positive life. This seems antithetical to your goal. That is not so much a question as an observation, but if you could elaborate on that, I would appreciate it.

HH: Mmmm, another very perceptive question. Thank you.

Our goal, is a Negative Harvest for Ourselves. Not for you. We provide the Catalyst of Negativity for you, and it is up to you what you do with it. The drastic extent of the Negativity we Create though, has more to do with us, than it does with you. Some of my earlier replies should make clear why that is so.

Also, in response to your observation regarding the antithetical nature of some of what I have shared here, there is a simple explanation.

Let's put it this way, I have already been, shall we say "chastised" for going well beyond my remit here. It was not intended that I be as open as I have been. In fact, if you follow the topic through again from the beginning, you may notice how my 'tone' toward you (collectively) has softened somewhat during our discourse together.

I have, as far as possible, adhered fully to the Laws of Free Will and Confusion, although there have been instances where I have said more than I should have. You yourselves will not suffer for this, however, when it comes to my next cycle in 4th Density Negative, and working off my Karmic Record, I will have to accept the consequences for my actions. But hey, I figure I've got a Negative enough life to come as it is, so what's a little extra going to matter.

I was reluctant to be the one tasked with this communication. I still very much have a 'weakness' for Compassion. But I obey and discharge the assignments given to me. **It has been a very long time, since I last spent any time in having direct dealings with 'your kind' in general. I do not mean that in an offensive way, just that the vast majority of my time, I only ever see Family during my daily and nightly tasks. I do not live what you would call a 'public' life. I am 'sheltered' and 'secluded'.**

I did not anticipate how involved I would become in this process. To be honest, I really did not expect so many questions, and such a warm and open minded reception (from the majority).

You could say, that I have in some way, grown somewhat 'attached' to you. In effect, this "Window of Opportunity, has also become such for me too. What began as me just doing my duty, has become more a 'labour of love', and when this is all over by the end of this evening, I think I will actually kind of miss you all, and having this involvement with those of the 'outside' world.

I was chosen because it was desired that someone of my "diplomacy" skills would be best to deliver this message. Due to the very nature of the subject matter, there was much potential for discord. It was felt important that the message did not become lost in a self righteous or defensive delivery system. So, you got me. And I'm actually glad now in retrospect that you did.

I sit here and chuckle to myself, (in light of the way some people here have spoken to me), how this discourse may have descended into something ugly, were certain others amongst my Family who were also considered for this assignment to have actually been given the job. Now I know why I was chosen. As with all things, it was meant to be this way. I couldn't care less what others think of me, so long as I know I am Serving my Creator as he desires, to the best of my ability. His is the only approval I require, or desire. I have nothing to defend, so I guess that's why I was 'perfect' for this task.

Anyway, enough with the sentiment, I have more questions to answer.

ATS: A common saying among Christians is "Satan's greatest trick is convincing the world that he didn't exist." I think there are Christians that would look at what you've written and see it as an elaborate ruse to "make the devil look good."

HH: **"Satan" is a human invention. Simply the 'personification' you have given to all the Negativity that has existed on this beautiful planet.** You didn't know who to 'blame', and as you could not find it within yourselves to take any of the responsibility, **"Satan" was created to absolve yourselves.**

ATS: Many of my friends and family are Christians, and they would likely think the same. How would one even go about presenting this information to a person of that mindset? I am not here to "spread your gospel", but I would definitely like so share this with a few of my friends.

HH: **How can you present anything to ones who have no desire to have their belief system challenged?**

They will believe what they want to believe, and noting you or I can say is likely to make any difference. It becomes ingrained at a subconscious level, and when a belief structure becomes that insidious, the only way it is likely to change, is through a 'mystical experience' or such a personal demonstration of 'another way' in the life lived of 'another', that one cannot fail but to notice that there is 'something different' about them. How can you reach such as these? **Only by example.**

ATS: That being said, is it okay if I condense your writings into one long post on my blog? I need to make sure that doesn't violate my user agreement here. I would also like to make sure that I won't get a visit from the men in black if I do so.

HH: That is amusing, thank you for the chuckle. Yes, you are most welcome to collate this discourse for presentation elsewhere. The only thing I ask, is that anyone chosing to do so, respects my wishes and copies only the message itself. In other words, do not include all the petty side discussion. If you want to present this message to others, please honour my (our) original intention, that the message is presented as a 'whole'. When I said in my opening post, that I required 'provisional faith' or 'suspended judgment', I made it very clear why this was the case.

I couldn't care less that people do not believe it. I never expected that many would. But what I desired, in asking for the above, was that the message was allowed to be presented in full, with all genuine questions replied to, and then once that process is complete, you can say whatever you like about how much of a hoax you may or may not believe it to be. If I may be crass for a brief moment, I couldn't give a "flying #" how much vitriol and scorn is poured upon our message, or how many futile verbal attacks may be launched against it's messenger. **The message will reach all those it is meant to reach, and that is exactly the way it should be. It is what the Creator wants. Those with ears to hear, eyes to see, and a heart to understand, will hear the message, and the seeds planted will grow strong in such fertile soil as these.**

So please therefore, if you respect that which I have shared here, and the courteous manner in which I have shared it, if you want to copy it, copy only my posts. My posts all quote within them the questions I respond to, so there are no other posts required, if a genuine representation of the message is that which you desire to take away with you.

ATS: Thank you for posting some of the most interesting information I have ever read. I am a bit of a crackpot and I scour the internet for conspiracies, alternative news, UFO videos and the like. I can't say I'm ready to completely buy what you're selling, but it has definitely resonated with me.

HH: You are welcome, and I in turn thank you, for reading it with an open mind.

I would never ask or expect you to 'buy' what I'm 'selling' If you notice, I have stated throughout our message, that the very last thing I want, is for it to be blindly believed, or taken as 'gospel'.

As I've said. It is yet another in a long line of "Catalysts", that your Infinite Creator has provided you with, down the course of history. **A Catalyst is not meant to be believed. It is meant to present you with a challenge to that which you "think" you know, about reality. And that is all it is meant to do.**

As always, how you respond to the Catalyst, is entirely up to you. Just the way it always should be.

Thank you very much for your very incisive and perceptive questions. Whether you realize it or not, you have contributed greatly to this discourse.

We wish you well, and ask our Infinite Creator to bless you, and guide your path.

ATS: H_H put out some incredibly well written information - **almost like it flowed from 'his/her' being onto the thread.**

HH: And that, is possibly the most perceptive realization in this discourse thus far.

It also allows me to respond further to an earlier question, that I indicated I would go into in more depth later, when replying to your observation.

This message does indeed "flow from my Being", onto the page.

I mentioned before, that my role in my Family, is that of the Spiritual Discipline.

A certain poster made all manner of assumptions as to what that role entails, and flailed wildly wide of the mark in the process.

As I said previously, all of the "Power Lines" (off world bloodlines) that comprise the "Inner Sanctum" (or "Hidden Hands") of the Family, have certain abilities that 3rd Density incarnates do not posses (even the others of our Family, the lines you know), one of these being the ability to know their entire incarnational 'past', with focussed concentration.

There are a wide array of tasks to be attended to, that allows our Family to function effectively, and we each specialize in certain areas or Disciplines, in order that the "body" of our Family runs like a well oiled machine.

My area, and that which I spend the vast majority of my time actively involved in, is that of Spirituality. OUR Spirituality, not that of the peoples of the Earth. Others below me deal more in that area.

I could be likened to that of a 'Priest' or a 'Minister'. In the same way as your religions and spiritual teachers have the responsibility of "listening" to the voice of their Creator, and delivering his messages, so to do I.

I have been actively engaged in this role now, for a great many years. It has become second nature to me. Actually, more accurately, it has become First nature. A large part of my role, is to constantly be in the awareness state of our Group Soul (Lucifer). That is why you will notice that I so often refer to "we" even as I am speaking in the first person. That has just become natural for me. I spend most of my time speaking with my Family, as Lucifer, the Group Soul perspective. When I speak henceforth, it is not me (the individual Soul spark) that is speaking to you in essence, but rather, for want of a better description, (because it is far from accurate), you could say that in effect, **I am "Channeling" Lucifer. That is why this discourse flows so easily. As some have noted, the chances of me having spent however much vast quantities of time "researching" all this material to "hoax" with, and present it in the fluent method that I do, as in regular daily installments, whilst I guess could be remotely possible, is unlikely in the extreme.**

For those who are open enough to receive the above explanation, now you know why, and how it is done. **I speak not for myself, but rather, for him who sent me, my own Creator (Lucifer).** I know and have experienced that which he knows and has experienced, because essentially, we are One and the same Being.

ATS: I have never been involved in any organized religions per say, but have always been spiritual. I do look at the many religious texts out there because I believe they all have parts to the story. One can find great knowledge from many different books or religious texts. I believe that we as humans are creators like the ONE creator and we are all one. I also believe we wil be moving into a higher level of consciousness where we can consciously co-create in our world, since we are only unconsciously co-creating at the moment.

HH: Your insight serves you well.

ATS: There is so much more I would like to speak with you about but am not able to think of what exactly I want to say. Thanks for those great words that you speak to us and appreciate what you are doing! With Love

HH: Do not worry friend, we feel your heart, and that does not need to be expressed via the confines of limited words. We can speak all you like, and will be happy to do so, when the Game is over.

ATS: Also do you know of **Miriam Delicado**? I just watched here interview on the project camelot site and it was very inspiring to me. So let me ask, are you one of the tall blondes that she speaks of.

HH: She is a beautiful Soul. I have not seen the interview of which you speak, but we know of her experiences. **The 'tall blondes' of which you speak, are of Plejaren heritage. They are working with what is know as the Galactic Confederation of Planets. They serve the Positive vibration. Plejarens are from the constellation you call the Pleiades. It's actual name is the Plejares, hence 'Plejarens'.**

And no, we are Lucifer, and nothing directly to do with the Plejarens, though they are indeed good friends of ours.

ATS: I have never seen a UFO or any of this spiritual stuff myself. I just know in my heart that it's there for me to find. **What can I do if anything to get myself in the correct frequency to see these things and have these experiences.** Any and all information you provide will be greatly appreciated.

HH: Simply believe, and know in your heart of their existence. Think about it. In all of this vast Creation, can you really believe that you are alone?

I will pre-warn you though, so as to avoid disappointment, **you will only receive communication from them, if that is something you have already agreed together in your Soul Contract before coming here.** Many here at this time (millions) have a part to play in the Great Awakening, and preparations for the Great Harvest. **Many who do not believe now, will begin to open their minds, as the Earth changes that are coming begin to take effect. People will be terrified, and have no idea what is going on, because the governments have concealed this information from you. These 'Travelers' or what some have termed "Star-Seeds" are incarnated here to help on the ground level, when this all begins play out, over the next few years. When the time is right, they will come forward.**

Most people are not ready to hear this information yet, but not so far off, they will be.

Many of these "Star Seeds" have not "awakened" yet themselves. The Confederation stands by ready to "help" them to do so, if it is necessary. For ones such as **these who have yet to "awaken", they will have felt all their lives that they are somehow "different", and they have a deep sense that somehow, they "do not belong here". Many of them will also have many dreams and even visions, of their lives on their Home planets. Many of these "Star Seeds", are in fact Plejaren. That is why the 'tall blondes' keep 'showing up'. To help their Family awaken to their assignments here.**

ATS: I am another of the many grateful forum members who appreciate the loving message given by Hidden_Hand. I wish I had discovered this thread before today. It's given me much comfort. I was running out of strength but now feel as though I might just be able to manage now. My gratitude is eternal. From this little spark to that one: Thanks for the light, mate.

HH: You are very welcome, we are glad to have been of Service. You actually 'feel' very familiar to me. If for the reasons I am feeling this to be the case, consider this message to you our part in our Soul Agreement fulfilled. Take the guidance in this message into your meditations, and also seek information from your Dreamtime. Test these words deeply, and take them into your heart, only if they 'feel' right, and truthful to you. If they do, then act upon them, and allow nothing or no-one to deter you. Arise and play the part that you volunteered to be here for right now. It is almost time. Prepare yourself, and be sure that you are ready.

We leave you with our strongest encouragement, and the love and Light of our One Infinite Creator.

ATS: He could be what he says he is i think. But he could be a well read but bored person wanting to see how far his hoax will spread on the internet.

The thing i do find is that if he is the latter it doesn't fit the profile. I mean if you read up on the stuff he obviously is interested in it is harder to wantingly hoax with it. It goes against the things he loves to read about. And i find it VERY hard to believe that he is researching this on the fly and putting all this work in something he will never get anymore 'fame' than this week of attention, no money or 'real life' recognition or whatever more.

HH: I was not going to respond to any more messages other than those who genuinely want to hear what we have to say, due to my fast expiring time here, though your point was poignant enough to briefly address, even if only that the accuracy of your statement deserves to have a place in the final collated version of this message. A LOT of work and pointless time wasted, were it not for the fact that this 'labour of love' is all done for the glory of our Creator. The lies and rumours about us being an 'evil' and 'satanic' Being have gone unanswered for far too long. It was time to set the record straight. Lucifer has sacrificed so much, because we love you.

ATS: As spirituality is your focus, could you comment on the role of the **Catholic church** in terms of your role and how the church fits in either the positive, negative, or miscellaneous paths?

HH: **The lower parts of our Family (the names you know) use the Vatican for many Rituals and**

Sacrifices. That should tell you all you need to know.

ATS: Any specific holy books (or perhaps Bible authors) you'd list as coming very close to the Truth?

HH: **The closet biblical authors, are those who have been 'left out' of the publicized editions.**

The closest "spiritual" writings (other than the Ra material) to containing truth about the nature of The One, are the Taoist writings, that of the 'Tao Te Ching', and the 'Book of Chuang Tzu'.

ATS: Greetings, Hidden Hand. I consider this a unique opportunity. I have not read this full thread but I have some detailed questions, so I apologize if something has already been answered. I want to make sure I get my questions out before your time expires.

HH: Almost all of your questions have been addressed, and those few which have not, I am sorry that I either am not permitted to speak on, or that due to the tiny amount of time I have left now, I cannot address. My apologies.

ATS: H-H, i hope you will answer my following questions.

You may be aware of me, as i also cannot reveal all that i know.

My question is of a different nature, which i cannot get answers to, My bloodline is of the elite, as to say. austrian count, english earl, scottish baron, It seems at some point in the last 100 years,one part of the family lost everything, taken from the government. There is alot i wish to say, but do not wish to tell for all to see. Are you aware of this happening? What really happened? The english side will not say, generations of family lived there, then taken by the government.....something happened. All in my family including myself have extensive abilities,myself seeming to have the most. I am also aware of all you have spoke of on here.
I would, if you have permission to do so, and i know this would be allowed due to this lineage, like to talk to you on a personal level.
Ask who you have to ask, you will see i am truthful and genuine.

Please do not see me as arrogant, but that is the only question i do not know.

HH: Obviously you understand, that these line you speak of are only the earthly lines, and we (off world Power lines) do not often intervene in such 'inter family') circumstances. All I am permitted to say, is that there was a dispute between the Hapsburg and Franco-Prussian lines. Things were said and done that should not have been. Consequences arose, and action was taken.

As for communication on a 'person' level, I am sorry this is not possible.

I hope that within the limits of that which I can say, you have the insight to connect the dots.

We wish you well in your tasks here, and will likely see you in the near future (if you are going to 'Malta in wintertime'?) No need to reply, as I will have taken my leave by then.

We shall deal with these next two posts together:

ATS 1: He is reptilian. That's the race of the bloodlines. They control just about everything behind the scenes
.

And remember there's no such thing as a bad race, just select individuals or groups who stand out more than others.

ATS 2: Ok so i have another question for hidden_hand. Reptilians are described as being very aggressive, arrogant and perceive humans to be nothing more than cattle. So what's with the split personalities? you're saying you are loving and spiritual and yet everyone says reptilians are fearsome beings?

HH: That amuses us. **We are most certainly NOT Reptilian, and there is nothing remotely reptilian about the True Power Bloodlines. The only 'Reptilian' influences that are in anyway remotely involved with this planet at this time, are those of the Zeta Reticuli and Alpha Draconis systems. They are of no particular threat to you.**

For those to whom it may be of some interest, **we are of Venusian heritage, originally. What is another name that Venus is called by? Connect the dots.**

Well, that is all the questions I promised to answer out of the way, and my time here is now pretty much expired. I have another few minutes before I must finish preparing for my long journey. There was two later posts, that I will just barely have time to offer a passing answer to:

ATS: I clearly know and are aware about this game…. But I have a question to you…..

Do your 3-d families have fractions. Do they not know this, all of them.

Because they have try to kill me, and it will not work. of course.

HH: All I can say on this, is that **even the Earthly lines of our "extended" Family, only know as much as we tell them. Certain information they may not use wisely, or with proper regard to our Creator, and our One Infinite Creator.**

As has been said before, "the top of the pyramid, is not the top of the pyramid".

Above the highest Earthline auspices of the Supreme World Council (and another higher aspect that cannot be named), are the "Hidden Hands" (not the real name of course, but what we have sometimes been referred to).

ATS: Yes, however the things/thoughts/ideas! he is speaking of are already a piece of copyrighted material and have been published in book format with ISBN numbers and all. The books are called the Law of One.
llresearch.org...

This/these books deal with the very same ideas as the OP:
1. Negative and positive polarization
2. Degrees of density
3. Even the same exact term: social memory complex!
4. harvest is used in the same context
5. Evolution between densities
6. Logos and sub-logos are used in the same context
7. The same concept of Wanderers
8. The concept of Infinity becoming aware of itself
9. The same idea of vibrations in the same context
10. The concept of 'us' progressing to the fourth density with the next harvest (2012) and how many of 'us' will have to repeat the third density.

There are well over 50 examples of the same ideas and contexts between the original author (L/L Research) and Hidden_Hand. L/L Research dates back to the 1981 timeframe, thereby leading me to believe that they are the original author. Again please note that the definition of plagiarism is the unauthorized use or close imitation of the language and thoughts of another author and the representation of them as one's own original work. Therefore, if Hidden_Hands is not with L/L Research he is clearly plagiarising their ideas and thoughts.

Sources [for numbered examples]:

www.llresearch.org...

www.llresearch.org...

www.llresearch.org...

www.llresearch.org...

www.llresearch.org...

ATS: Even Lucifer had to step in to help me. That was a surprise as you can understand.

Does your left hand dont know what the right hand teach. Or is it lack of understanding in certain members in your bloodline.

HH: Indeed, I understand, occasionally drastic intervention is required. As I said, they do not know everything, somethings are best kept to ourselves. Temptation can prove too great, when certain Powers lay in the hands of those who's Heart is not utterly Pure of intention. Let us just say, that some seem to enjoy the game a little TOO much, from time to time.

Their actions were more from ignorance, than malicious intent toward you. Please forgive them, as they knew not what they were doing, but thought it the right thing.

Ok, I've just finished reading the last few pages of questions, I stated now on a few occasions that I have no time left to answer, but I was asked earlier a question that I said I'd finish with, namely that of "if there was a question you had not yet been asked yet, would you consider this it being asked", or words to that effect.

So there is one other question from the last pages that I will use in that vein.

This will really have to be it though. I am truly sorry I cannot reply to the many other heartfelt responses that sadly must remain unanswered. We must be leaving for an important task in Rome, and already I have others here with me imploring me "will you please just shut down that flipping computer and get your things together". They are laughing at how 'involved' I have become in this task of mine. My Father is teasing that I should begin at early 6th Density again to balance my compassion. Anyway, I must finish:

ATS: This has been very informative, and has cleared up much for me. Thanks once again, Hidden_Hand. My take on this is much different even from what it was the last time I posted in this thread. So, hopefully these questions will be a little more relevant...

1) I am curious as to how the bloodline family structure works. You said there are people who are part of your "extended family" that we may know of. So are these the Rockefeller, Rothschild, Bush, House of Windsor, etc. (typically known in conspiracy circles as the New World Order?). How close is your interaction with your "extended family" and are they as spiritually enlightened as you seem to be? Can you just kind of give us an outline of how the family is structured, how much each level knows in relation to the top, etc.? Because there are a lot of theories and "know-it-alls" out there, and it would be nice to get it straight once and for all. Be as detailed as you feel is appropriate.

HH: Ok, and this will have to be a really brief overview, as my time is up.

Starting at the bottom level, you have what we call **"Local Cell Groups" or "Family Clusters"**. There will be anything from say five to thirty or so of these, depending upon the size of the town or city in question. Each Local area has it's own Council, comprised of Local Leaders representing the Six Disciplines of learning. There is also either a High Priest or High Priestess of The Order, who Serves their local community.

Above this, you have the **Regional Council**, with the Leader of each Local Council representing their specific areas. Then the **National Council**, in the same vein, with the Leaders of the Regional Councils sitting to represent their Regions.

Then you have the **Supreme World Council** above them all, with the National Leaders representing their Countries. **Above this, is another group I cannot mention, who liaise with the "Hidden Hands"**.

Then above this, there are many other levels of Leadership, purely from the Power Lines (the ones that are not of this planet). The Supreme World Council, only know as much as is "Handed" down to them from us.

In our Power Lines, we have a similar structure, with Local and Regional groups etc, though most of us are living in entirely 'different' types of communities than you would understand. All I shall say is that **we are not "surface dwellers"**.

ATS: ...also, do people ever try to leave the family? I asked you to comment on the case of one "**Svali**" in an earlier post. I am still curious if she was one of you or your extended family, or is she just a mis/disinfo agent.

HH: I am aware of her, yes. I've not looked at her supposed "revelations" personally, though heard enough from others in my Family. Yes, **she was a part of the Family, at the lower levels**, from the German Lines I believe. As I understand, she did reveal **a lot of truth about the lower levels**, but she was only Regional Level in the Earth Lines, so not that high. She certainly would not have had anything like the "bigger picture". I understand that she went into detail about some of the **training techniques in the lower levels, which to be fair, can be extremely harsh, though as I've said, it's all about reaching the 95% Negativity**, and when all is said and done, no matter how much one may have suffered in this life-experience, we can never lose sight of the fact that **this is a Game we are all playing here together, and each incarnating Soul has already chosen and agreed in advance the parts they will play in the Game**. No one really suffers, except in the Game, and ultimately, they have chosen these experiences before hand, at a Soul level. **No one is 'forced' to incarnate into a storyline they do not want to play and learn from.**

The German House is renowned for being particularly harsh and severe in it's training, so much of what she shares may have happened, though my Family have also said that unless her "trainers" were acting "out of protocol" (abusing their power) much of what she 'revealed' would not have happened, or has been embellished to some degree, for whatever reason. I cannot comment myself, as I've had neither the time or inclination to examine her story. The world of my own Family is very different from that of the lower Earth based bloodlines. **Whilst our (my own) training growing up was very strict and disciplined, we were never abused in any way. We grew up with the bigger picture, and didn't need any other motivation.**

The Earth lines are not aware of the entire picture. They themselves are not of our Lucifer Group Soul, and as far as they are aware, they are out to 'rule the world', to Control and Enslave, and create as much Suffering and Negativity as is humanly possible. That's what they 'get out of the deal'. World Domination. You'd have to say with that in mind, they're doing a great job. But one of the things they don't know or understand, is that our (Venusian Power Lines) agenda, is ultimately for the Highest Good of all concerned, in providing you with the Catalyst. **If they were aware of this Truth, there is a slight risk that they would not have done their jobs properly, and they would miss out on joining us in our 95% Negative Harvest. They are aware of the Harvest, and the need for them to attain the 95%, to get out of 3rd Density, and that is all the motivation they need to help us achieve our ultimate aims.**

How they go about it, is not really of too great a concern to us, as long as they are getting the job done. Sometimes we have to step in, where something they may do or plan goes against our desires, but such instances are few and far between.

And with that, I absolutely have to finish my time here with you. If I leave it any longer, I am going to be late for my journey, and I will not be very popular if I make my Family late. It is a strange feeling I have now in my heart, as I write these last few lines. I never could have imagined I would have 'connected' with you all in this way through this discourse. It was never the original intention, just to put out the information required of me. But somewhere along this journey we have taken together, I have come to feel a certain 'bond' with you. Of course, I know that bond is our inherent Unity in our One Infinite Creator, though, to have kind of 'met' and connected personally with so many of you, has left me feeling somewhat saddened that our time has to come to end. But come to an end it must.

I thank you sincerely for your gracious hospitality, and for allowing us to 'use' your 'space' here, for the furthering of our message. And remember, no matter the ideologies that may separate us in this Game, the message is all that matters, and the message is, that in the Love, and the Light of our Infinite Creator, we are All One. Brother's and Sisters of the Light.

We wish you all the very best in what remains of your journeys here, and sincerely hope for you that you will use the Catalyst we have offered you, to in some way help you to Graduate with a glorious and Positive Great Harvest.

Me on the other hand, I'm going to have to go and do some REALLY Negative things now to make up for all this Positivity. Kind of amusing, in an ironic way.

I look forward to meeting up with so many of you when the Game is over, and enjoying reminiscing about this time, and the parts we have all played in this Great Game.

We leave you all in the Love, and the Light of our One Infinite Creator.

Namasté.

Endnotes:

[1] ^ "Houses" is exactly what mind control survivor Svali talked about in an interview with Greg Szymanski in July 2006. See my article, *"The Illuminati Organization Structure, According to Illuminati Programmer, Svali"*.

[2] ^ This link leads to a few years old article of mine, where I emphasize that the only way to win this battle is to increase your spiritual awareness. This guy is saying the same thing. *Wes*

CPSIA information can be obtained
at www.ICGtesting.com
Printed in the USA
LVHW020245120121
676222LV00044B/1645